ENGLISH FOUNDATIONS

By

PATRICK JOSEPH HESSION

ISBN: 978-0-6151-9782-1

TABLE OF CONTENTS

ABOUT THIS BOOK

ENGLISH FOUNDATIONS was written for anyone who is enrolled in a G.E.D., intermediate or advanced ESL, remedial, developmental, or home school program. It is written for anyone who has ever had trouble mastering English grammar. This includes housewives, secretaries, and business people, as well as recent high school graduates. If you were left behind somewhere along the way toward mastering the basics of our language, this book is for you!

It is entirely <u>self-paced</u> and <u>self-grading</u>. You can take as much or as little time as you need to understand and master the rules. You can take it section by section, or you can review only those sections that gave you the most trouble. You are the boss!

It may come as a surprise, and even a shock, to discover that English really does have rules that work the same way all the time, once you understand the simple clues. Each part of speech has its own particular job to do that no other par of speech can do – much like parts in a car or pieces in a puzzle. Once you learn what the description and purpose of each part of speech is, you will be able to identify and use it correctly every time. It may help to visualize a noun, for instance, as an apple, and a proper noun as a Red Delicious apple; a verb as a pear; a pronoun as a peach, etc. One can never be the other, but together they make a pretty tasty dish!

You can grade yourself as you go along by simply *dividing the number you got right by the Possible Score* for the exercise you are doing. Example, if you got 14 right out of 16 (Possible Score), divide 14 by 16 and you will get a percent (88%). That will be *Your Score*. All of the correct answers are found after the review section of each Foundation. If you find that your score isn't as good as you would like for the first exercise, go back and review the rules and see what you don't understand. Then try the next exercise. Continue this until you are satisfied with yourself. When you are satisfied, try the Application. I am sure that the review of the Foundation will prove to you that you have finally mastered that part of speech once and for all!

I had the opportunity to preview this book with a Written Communication class I taught at IVY Tech State College in Indiana. The class included several older students as well as a woman from India and a woman from Saudi Arabia. I am grateful to these students for their corrections and suggestions and have incorporated them. To them this book is dedicated.

COMMENTS FROM STUDENTS

"I found it to be of help as a supplement to the other material...the material itself was written in a clear, understandable form." Eric Dolch

"I thought it was self-explanatory and thorough. I have difficulty with reading explanations and understanding but, for the most part, I understood what you were directing us to do. Your ENGLISH FOUNDATIONS covered the parts of speech that are essential to us all." Patricia Keeling

"There were sections that were really difficult for me to understand. I think this was due to my age more than anything else. You see, I have been out of school for better than 25 years...I think this will be a great teaching tool." Betty Knox

"In regards to your book, ENGLISH FOUNDATIONS, I found it to be very rewarding, informative, and useful. I feel that you have spent a great deal of time in the preparation of this book, and, in my opinion, I feel it has paid off." Charlotte Robbins

"At first, I thought some of Foundations could have been explained in more detail, but, as I went along, it got easier. I feel the reason I was having a hard time understanding it is because I've been out of school for 13 years. Overall, I feel the book was helpful and easy to understand." Linda Campbell

"I found it helpful and easy to understand." Madhuri Dubey, India

"It was good." Amal Engrees, Saudi Arabia

ENGLISH FOUNDATIONS

FOUNDATION I

NOUNS

A **NOUN** is any person, place, thing, idea, or quality. It answers the question **WHO**? or **WHAT?**

Example: Book, song, John, happiness, sunshine

PROPER NOUNS refer to a **PARTICULAR** person, place, or thing, not just any ordinary one. To show this, they ordinarily should be capitalized, like John above. Sometimes, however, the noun is not capitalized, but the particular word that describes it is.

Example: We went to the White Mountains during our vacation. (Not just any mountains, but particular mountains.)

Example: Albert Einstein was a great scientist. (Not just any man, but a particular man.)

Example: Fraser Firs originated in North Carolina mountains.

EXERCISE 1. Underline, and capitalize as necessary, the Proper noun or nouns in the following sentences. (Possible score: 21)

1. pat owns a flaming red mazda.

2. We visited the empire state building.

3. I enjoy eating at the red lobster.

4. We visited our relatives at christmas time.

5. The israelites crossed the red sea to freedom.

6. miss johnson is our secretary.

7. In wisconsin, there are many dairies.

8. My children like to watch sesame street in the morning.

9. The statue of liberty is located in new york.

10. anne is out picking berries.

Answers are on page 21. Subtract one point for each incorrect answer. *Your Score:* ____

EXERCISE 2. <u>Underline, and capitalize as necessary,</u> the <u>Proper noun</u> or <u>nouns</u> in the following sentences. (Possible score: 30)

1.   The poem *beowolf* is anglo-saxon, but it is not native to english soil.

2.   With christianity, a new spirit entered into english poetry.

3.   bede's last work was the translation of st. john's gospel into english.

4.   The next great name in literature after king alfred is aelfric.

5.   The most distinguished name in the literature of the 14th. century is that of geoffrey chaucer.

6.   In addition to his dramas, shakespeare wrote two long narrative poems and 154 sonnets.

7.   sir francis bacon was the greatest prose writer of his age.

8.   The great literature of the elizabethan age was in poetry.

9.   john milton is usually regarded as the second greatest name in english literature.

10.   A notable name in the puritan age is that of john bunyan, who wrote *pilgrim's progress*.

Answers are on page 21. Subtract one point for each incorrect answer. *Your Score:* _____

EXERCISE 3. <u>Underline, and capitalize as necessary</u> the <u>Proper noun</u> or <u>nouns</u> in the following sentences. (Possible score: 18)

1.   The sumerians were a non-semitic people who migrated into the fertile Mesopotamian valley before 4000 B.C.

2.   The oldest sumerian inscriptions are short, historical in character, and were probably composed shortly after 4000 B.C.

3.   semites from the southwest also settled in mesopotamia.

4.   Gradually they conquered and absorbed their sumerian neighbors.

5.   The babylonian people resulted from this fusion.

6. The babylonian language was semitic, but the superior sumerian civilization prevailed.

7. sumarian survived for over thirty centuries as the language of religious documents.

8. The semetic babylonian, or akkadian as it is commonly called, became the language of daily life and profane literature.

9. sumerian cuneiform writing was used in all babylonian documents.

10. The great babylonian period lasted from about the 22nd. to the 13th. century B.C.

Answers are on page 21. Subtract one point for each incorrect answer. *Your Score*: _____

APPLICATION. Write 5 sentences using Proper nouns. Underline the Proper noun or nouns in each sentence.

1._____

2._____

3._____

4._____

5._____

COMMON NOUNS refer to a class, or individual units of a class of persons, places, things, ideas, or qualities.

   Example: Many tourists visit the mountains in the summertime.

   Example: My house is located on a quiet street.

   Example: Happiness is a warm feeling.

EXERCISE 1. Underline the Common noun or nouns in the following sentences. (Possible score: 22)

1. My pen is out of ink.

2. Let me help you with the dishes.

3.	Joe rides his motorcycle to work every day.

4.	The ideas of beauty and goodness are hard to put into words.

5.	Sunshine is the life-blood of life on earth.

6.	Tragedy struck suddenly when the plane crashed.

7.	The King reins in his horse.

8.	When I get to my house, I'm going straight to bed.

9.	The heel of my shoe is wearing down.

10.	John says that his dog does not have a scent.

Answers are on page 22. Subtract one point for each incorrect answer. *Your Score:* ____

EXERCISE 2. Underline the Common noun or nouns in the following sentences.
(Possible score: 29)

1.	The great Babylonian period lasted from about the 22nd. to the 13th. century B.C.

2.	Then, the Assyrians, a kindred people, succeeded to power.

3.	Among them, conquest and power were held in high honor.

4.	The works of culture didn't mean much.

5.	As a result, their literary work shows little originality.

6.	They copied the Babylonian writings and preserved them in libraries.

7.	The library in Nineveh contained about 30,000 clay tablets.

8.	This library was our first great source of information about Babylonian literature.

9.	It contained histories, grammars, lexicons, mathematics, and poems.

10.	With the fall of Nineveh, the library was buried in the ruins of the palace.

Answers are on page 22. Subtract one point for each incorrect answer. *Your Score*: ____

EXERCISE 3. Underline the Common noun or nouns in the following sentences. (Possible score: 25)

1.   A famous Babylonian epic tells the story of creation.

2.   Marduk, the great god, slays Tiamat, the dragon of chaos.

3.   Out of one half of her body he forms the heavens.

4.   Out of the other half he forms the earth.

5.   He then creates plants, animals, and man on earth.

6.   This story is strikingly similar to the biblical Creation story.

7.   It is likely that borrowing took place.

8.   The epic is arranged in seven tablets, corresponding to the seven days of the week.

9.   Of equal literary and historical importance is the Code of Hammurabi, a king of Babylon about 2100 B.C.

10.   It contains almost 300 laws and is probably the oldest legal code in history.

Answers are on page 22. Subtract one point for each incorrect answer. *Your Score*: _____

APPLICATION. Write 5 sentences using Common nouns. Underline the common noun in each sentence.

1._____

2._____

3_____

4._____

5._____

An **ABSTRACT NOUN** describes a quality, attribute, or concept. You can't see, touch, or feel it, but you know that it exists, and you can talk about it.

Example: Love is a many-splendored thing.

Example: She was filled with sadness at the loss of her mother.

Example: The <u>family</u> is the basic <u>unit</u> of <u>society</u>.

EXERCISE 1. <u>Underline</u> the <u>Abstract</u> <u>noun</u> or <u>nouns</u> in the following sentences.
(Possible score: 17)

1.   Clear paragraphs require unity, coherence, and emphasis.

2.   The early morning sunrise filled me with joy and ecstasy.

3.   We respond better to friendliness than to hostility.

4.   I asked my mother for forgiveness.

5.   The fullness of the moon lit up the night.

6.   My first impression of Janice was a pleasant one.

7.   The Statue of Liberty is a symbol of our democracy.

8.   We fight for the ideas of freedom, liberty, and brotherhood.

9.   Economic freedom is one of the most precious gifts we possess.

10.   Job satisfaction is becoming more difficult.

Answers are on page 23. Subtract one point for each incorrect answer. *Your Score:* _____

EXERCISE 2. <u>Underline</u> the <u>Abstract</u> <u>noun</u> or <u>nouns</u> in the following sentences.
(Possible score: 38)

1.   Families vary in organization, membership, ideologies, and other functions.

2.   Indeed, the definition of marriage is not the same across cultures.

3.   Family members with different perspectives may find themselves in bitter
        conflict.

4.   To question the idea of a happy family is not to say that love and joy are not
        present.

5.   Also, people find their deepest satisfaction in their families.

6.   Rather, the happy family assumption omits important aspects of family life.

7.   Literature and drama portray families charged with love and hate, tenderness and spite.

8.   Family violence seems to be a product of psychological tensions and external stresses.

9.   Children come into the world with unique temperaments and other characteristics.

10.   Children are active agents in the construction of knowledge about the world.

Answers are on page 23. Subtract one point for each incorrect answer. *Your Score:* _____

EXERCISE 3. Underline the Abstract noun or nouns in the following sentences. (Possible score: 21)

1.   The family provides the framework for all pre-state society and the fount of its creativeness.

2.   In groping for survival and knowledge, human beings learned to control their sexual desires.

3.   They learned to suppress their individual selfishness, aggression, and competition.

4.   The other side of this self-control was increased capacity for love.

5.   Civilization would have been impossible without this initial self-control, seen in incest prohibitions and in the generosity and moral orderliness of primitive family life.

Answers are on page 23. Subtract one point for each incorrect answer. *Your Score:* _____

APPLICATION. Write 5 sentences using Abstract nouns. Underline the abstract noun or nouns in each sentence.

1._____

2._____

3._____

4._____

5._____

A **CONCRETE NOUN** describes something in a form that you can see, hear, touch, smell, taste, or feel. It is material.

    Example: I am going to wash my <u>car</u> today.

    Example: The apple <u>pie</u> smells delicious.

Exercise 1. <u>Underline</u> the <u>Concrete</u> <u>noun</u> or <u>nouns</u> in the following sentences. (Possible score: 18)

1.   The wind was howling through the trees.

2.   We are having a picnic in the park today.

3.   Germs cause sickness.

4.   Don't damage your eyes by looking at the sun.

5.   After the snowstorm, the roads were very icy.

6.   The boys have a chance to win their football game.

7.   How much are those shoes?

8.   The room echoed with the sound of music.

9.   I need to get my purse out of the trunk.

10.   Wiping up paint isn't much fun.

Answers are on page 24. Subtract one point for each incorrect answer. *Your Score*: _____

Exercise 2. <u>Underline</u> the <u>Concrete</u> <u>noun</u> or <u>nouns</u> in the following sentences. (Possible score: 12)

1.   Hebrew literature began, like almost every other ancient literature, in folk songs and legends.

2.   These were probably recited in camps and village gatherings by tribal bards.

3.   Some of these poems were written down.

4.   The Bible mentions two collections of ancient Hebrew songs.

5.   Unfortunately, only a few fragments of these ancient poems survive.

Answers are on page 24. Subtract one point for each incorrect answer. *Your Score*: ____

Exercise 3. Underline the Concrete noun or nouns in the following sentences. (Possible score: 15)

1.   The Bible makes up the sacred book of Christian peoples.

2.   The Jews regard only the Old Testament books as sacred.

3.   The Bible is a collection of books, a small library.

4.   Therefore, it contains many kinds of writings, including historical sketches and unhistorical or semi-historical legends, and religious and social laws.

5.   It also contains the inspired utterances and visions of the prophets, liturgical and lyric poems, didactic poetry, pragmatic fiction, and even a pure love poem.

Answers are on page 24. Subtract one point for each incorrect answer. *Your Score*: ____

APPLICATION. Write 5 sentences using Concrete nouns. Underline the concrete noun or nouns in each sentence.

1._____

2._____

3._____

4._____

5._____

A **COLLECTIVE NOUN** describes a group or collection of persons or things as one unit.

        Example: Our team is the best in the league.

        Example: The cast is rehearsing for a new play.

EXERCISE 1. Underline the Collective noun or nouns in the following sentences. (Possible score: 14)

1.   Our school has a good spirit of enthusiasm and cooperation.

2.   My company builds its reputation on honesty.

3.   The army is looking for men and women of character.

4.   Are you going to the circus when it comes to our town?

5.   Many people look forward to the evening news.

6.   Citrus fruit provides many needed vitamins.

7.   We expect a bumper crop this year.

8.   The McCarthy family moved into our neighborhood today.

9.   The crowd rose to its feet as the team scored a touchdown.

10.   The crew of an airline usually consists of a pilot, co-pilot, and several flight attendants.

Answers are on page 24. Subtract one point for each incorrect answer. *Your Score*: _____

EXERCISE 2. Underline the Collective noun or nouns in the following sentences. (Possible score: 9)

1.   The oldest biblical writings are found in the Pentateuch and in Judges and Samuel.

2.   Scientists have established that the Pentateuch was composed by different writers between 900 B.C. and 400 B.C., or even somewhat later.

3.   It has proved also that the book of Joshua was composed by these same writers.

4.   Following these oldest writings came the so-called Yahwist and Elohist documents.

5.   They were composed in the Southern and the Northern Kingdoms respectively.

Answers are on page 24. Subtract one point for each incorrect answer. *Your Score*: _____

EXERCISE 3. Underline the Collective noun or nouns in the following sentences.
(Possible score: 9)

1.   The Yahwist document is so-called by scholars because it uses only the name
        Yahweh for God.

2.   The Elohist document is likewise so designated because it uses the word Elohim
        for God.

3.   The vast majority of the narratives of Genesis, Exodus, Numbers, and Joshua
        belong to the Yahwist and Elohist documents.

4.   The study of the Bible is a very interesting but sometimes difficult undertaking.

5.   However, understanding these writings is important for understanding many of
        our current laws and customs.

Answers are on page 24. Subtract one point for each incorrect answer. *Your Score*: ____

APPLICATION: Write 5 sentences using Collective nouns. Underline the collective
noun or nouns in each sentence.

1._____

2._____

3._____

4._____

5._____

A **COMPOUND NOUN** is a noun made up of two or more words. Some are written as
separate words. Some have hyphens (-) between the words. Some are written as a single
word.

        Example: My father-in-law works at the Post Office.

        Example: I received a new ballpoint pen for Christmas.

        Example: We receive the morning and Sunday newspaper.

-12-

EXERCISE 1. <u>Underline</u> the <u>Compound</u> <u>noun</u> or <u>nouns</u> in the following sentences. (Possible score: 16)

1.   The recipe calls for one cupful of sugar.

2.   The Secretary-General of the United Nations was in Washington.

3.   I like pancakes with either honey or maple syrup.

4.   We gave my brother-in-law a new motorboat to fish with.

5.   There is a wide gap between the "haves" and the "have-nots".

6.   Native Americans have been mistreated for the most part.

7.   Most businessmen are members of the Chamber of Commerce.

8.   The passer-by seemed to be in quite a hurry.

9.   Joe Stewart is the new President-elect of our club.

10.   The playground was filled with schoolgirls and schoolboys.

Answers are on page 25. Subtract one point for each incorrect answer. *Your Score*: _____

EXERCISE 2. <u>Underline</u> the <u>Compound</u> <u>noun</u> or <u>nouns</u> in the following sentences. (Possible score: 5)

1.   Language, spoken and written, is mankind's most valuable asset.

2.   A rich inheritance of language belongs to the English-speaking nations.

3.   The works of scholars, poets, story-tellers, orators, and scientists have contributed much to our literature.

4.   This has resulted in free discussion of political questions and in wide circulation of books, magazines, and newspapers.

5.   English has become universally recognized as a world language just as Latin once was.

Answers are on page 25. Subtract one point for each incorrect answer. *Your Score*: _____

EXERCISE 3. Underline the Compound noun or nouns in the following sentences. (Possible score: 5)

1.   "Friends, Romans, countrymen, lend me your ears."

2.   My sister received an award for safe-conduct.

3.   A sturdy lock is a safeguard against theft.

4.   Many people cruised the oceans on the *Queen Mary*.

5.   Thousands of people visit the Lincoln Memorial in Washington, D.C. every year.

Answers are on page 25. Subtract one point for each incorrect answer. *Your Score*: _____

APPLICATION: Write 5 sentences using Compound nouns. Underline the compound noun or nouns in each sentence.

1._____

2._____

3._____

4._____

5._____

Nouns differ from each other by their sex or **GENDER**. Nouns that refer to males are said to be of the **MASCULINE** gender.

Example: My father is sixty-five years old.

Example: My brother and I are the only boys in our family.

Nouns that refer to females are said to be of the **FEMININE** gender.

Example: His mother was a woman of outstanding courage.

Example: My wife and her sister went to the movies.

Nouns that name things that aren't male or female are said to be of the **NEUTER** gender.

Example: I just bought a new <u>house</u> this week.

Example: <u>Peaches</u> and <u>apples</u> are two of my favorite <u>fruits</u>.

Nouns that could be either male or female, or both, are said to be of the **COMMON** gender.

Example: <u>Horses</u> are Anne favorite <u>animal</u>.

Example: There are too many <u>students</u> in our class.

Gender may be shown by changing the word.

Example: <u>rooster</u> (male) to <u>hen</u> (female).

Example: <u>man</u> (male) to <u>woman</u> (female).

Gender may be shown by adding a word.

Example: <u>servant</u> (common) to <u>manservant</u> (male)

Example: <u>in-laws</u> (common) to <u>mother-in-law</u> (female)

Gender may be shown by suffixes.

Example: <u>hero</u> (male) to <u>heroine</u> (female)

Example: <u>deacon</u> (male) to <u>deaconess</u> (female).

EXERCISE 1. <u>Underline</u> each <u>noun</u> in the following sentences. <u>Place</u> an **M** above it if it is <u>male</u>, **F** if it is <u>female</u>, **N** if it is <u>neuter</u>, or **C** if it is <u>common</u>. (Possible Score: 50)

1.   Many people keep their homes cooler in the summertime.

2.   Summer vacations are times of great fun.

3.   The oil in our car keeps leaking.

4.   There is a new industry in our town.

5.   There weren't any injuries in the accident.

6.   The doctor gave treatments to the child.

7.   The clown amuses many people.

8.   In a pasture of cows there is usually only one bull.

9.   The girls and boys were freezing outside during recess.

10.   The snake kept trying to strike at me.

Answers are on page 25   Subtract one point for each incorrect answer. *Your Score* _____

EXERCISE 2. In the following sentences, <u>show the gender by changing a word, by adding a word,</u> or <u>by using a suffix.</u> (Possible Score: 5)

1.   My father-in-law (   ) and I enjoy listening to music.

2.   We have fifteen chickens (   ) in the barnyard.

3.   The Morning Show now has a new host (   ).

4.   The Prince (   ) is going to the ball.

5.   Jean was an intelligent man (   ).

Answers are on page 25. Subtract one point for each incorrect answer. *Your Score* _____

APPLICATION. Write 10 sentences using the rules above. Underline each noun and indicate its gender by the symbols used in Exercise 1.

1._____

2._____

3._____

4._____

5._____

6._____

7._____

8._____

9._____

10._____

Nouns differ from each other according to **PERSON**. The **FIRST PERSON** is the person who is speaking. The **SECOND PERSON** is the person or thing spoken to. The **THIRD PERSON** is the person or thing spoken about.

    Example: I, John Wilson, am running for President.

    Example: Judy, you have just been selected Queen of the Sweetheart Ball.

    Example: The new teacher excited her class with her enthusiasm.

EXERCISE. Show the person of the underlined nouns in the following sentences by placing a **1**, **2**, or **3** over each. (Possible Score: 10)

1.   Dad, may I go on your next trip with you?

2.   The soup today was especially tasty.

3.   What are you baking, Mary?

4.   I, the valiant hunter, will save you from the lion.

5.   Mother, may I have a cookie?

6.   John, go to the Post Office and mail this letter.

7.   The car will be repaired in about three hours.

8.   Abraham Lincoln was President of the United States.

9.   Mike is out wading in the pool.

10.   I, the Lord, am your God.

Answers are on page 25. Subtract one point for each incorrect answer. *Your Score* _____

APPLICATION. Write 6 sentences using each person twice.

1._____

2._____

3._____

4._____

5._____

6._____

Nouns differ from each other by their **NUMBER**.

If a noun refers to one person, place, or thing, it is said to be **SINGULAR** (singular number).

Example: Throw me the <u>ball</u>.

Example: Make sure your <u>child</u> gets plenty of rest.

If a noun refers to more than one person, place, or thing, it is said to be **PLURAL** (plural number).

Example: There are many <u>birds</u> in that tree.

Example: Sweet <u>strawberries</u> are my favorite dessert.

EXERCISE. <u>Underline</u> the <u>noun</u> or <u>nouns</u> in the following sentences. <u>Put a **P**</u> over each noun that is <u>plural</u>, and an <u>**S**</u> over each noun that is <u>plural</u>. (Possible Score: 40)

1.   The children were playing in the yard.

2.   Always obey red danger signs at railroad crossings.

3.   I need to practice my handwriting.

4.   On the way to the store, I found two dimes.

5.   Just before the bell rang, I finished my homework.

6.   Did you find the maps?

7.   The secretaries typed a large stack of letters.

8.   The two nations agreed on a peace treaty.

9.   Some people have great ability to do many things.

10.   Be careful with the laptop computer

Answers are on page 25. Subtract one point for each incorrect answer. *Your Score* ____

APPLICATION. Write five sentences using singular and plural nouns. Put a **P** over each noun that is plural and an **S** over each noun that is singular.

1._____

2._____

3._____

4._____

5._____

REVIEW OF FOUNDATION I

EXERCISE 1. After each noun below, put a check in the proper place if it is a Proper, Common, Abstract, Concrete, Collective, or Compound noun. (Possible Score: 12)

NOUN PROPER COMMON ABSTRACT CONCRETE COLLECTIVE COMPOUND

Rosebud

Alaska

Americans

Safety

Homework

Women

Ann

Team

Football

Cow

Skill

Man

Answers are on page 26. Subtract one point for each incorrect answer. *Your Score* ____

EXERCISE 2. In the sentences below, put a **P** over each proper noun and a **C** over each common noun. (Possible score: 25)

1. Each day, several thousand people visit the lincoln memorial in washington.

2. The monument was designed by henry bacon and was dedicated on memorial day.

3. Located in west potomac park, the lincoln memorial consists of a large marble hall which encloses a lifelike statue of abraham lincoln.

4. The figure, which was made from twenty-eight blocks of white marble by Daniel chester french, a distinguished sculptor, is sitting in a large armchair as if in deep meditation.

5. On the north wall is found a famous passage from an inaugural address by lincoln, and on the south wall is inscribed the gettysburg address.

Answers are on page 26. Subtract one point for each incorrect answer. *Your Score* ____

EXERCISE 3. Over each of the nouns in the sentences below, put a **PRO** if it is proper, **COM** if it is common, **CON** if it is concrete, **ABS** if it is abstract, **COL** if it is collective, and **COMP** if it is compound. (Possible Score: 39)

1. Friends, Romans, countrymen, lend me your ears; I come to bury Caesar, not to praise him. --William Shakespeare

2. The best laid schemes o' mice and o' men often go wrong. --Robert Burns

3. My heart leaps up when I behold a rainbow in the sky. --William Wordsworth

4. A thing of beauty is a joy forever. --John Keats

5. It was many and many a year ago,

   In a kingdom by the sea,

   That a maiden there lived whom you may know

   By the name of Annebel Lee. --Edgar Allan Poe

6. Hitch your wagon to a star. --Ralph Waldo Emerson

7. And the night shall be filled with music.

   And the cares that infest the day

   Shall fold their tents, like the Arabs,

   And as silently steal away. --Henry Wadsworth Longfellow

8. The paths of glory lead but to the grave. --Thomas Gray

9. My object in life is to write;

   My avocation and my vocation. --Robert Frost

10. The quality of mercy is not strained.

    It drops as the gentle rain from heaven

    Upon the place beneath. --William Shakespeare

Answers are on page 26. Subtract one point for each incorrect answer. *Your Score* _____

ANSWERS TO FOUNDATION I

PROPER NOUNS

Exercise 1	**Exercise 2**	**Exercise 3**
Pat	Beowolf	Sumarians
Mazda	Anglo-Saxon	non-Semetic people
Empire State Building	English soil	Mesopotamian valley
Red Lobster	Christianity	Sumarian inscriptions
Christmas	English poetry	Semites

Israelites
Red Sea
Miss Johnson
Wisconsin
Sesame Street
Statue of Liberty
New York
Anne

Bede
St. John's (Gospel)
English
King Alfred
Aelfric
Geoffrey Chaucer
Shakespeare
Sir Francis Bacon
Elizabethan Age
John Milton
English literature
Puritan Age
John Bunyan
Pilgrim's Progress

Mesopotamia
Sumarian neighbors
Babylonian people
Babylonian language
Semitic
Sumarian civilization
Sumarian
Semitic Babylonian
Akkadian
Sumarian cuneiform writing
Babylonian document
Babylonian period

COMMON NOUNS

Exercise 1
pen
ink
dishes
motorcycle
work
day
beauty
goodness
words
Sunshine
life-blood
life
earth
Tragedy
plane
horse
house
bed
heel
shoe
dog
scent

Exercise 2
period
century
people
power
conquest
power
honor
works
culture
result
work
originality
writings
libraries
library
tablets
library
source
information
literature
histories
grammars
lexicons
mathematics
poems

Exercise 3
epic
creation
god
dragon
chaos
half
body
heavens
half
earth
plants
animals
man
earth
story
story
borrowing
epic
tablets
days
week
importance
laws
code
history

fall
library
ruins
palace

ABSTRACT NOUNS

Exercise 1

unity
coherence
emphasis
joy
ecstasy
friendliness
hostility
forgiveness
fullness
impression
democracy
freedom
liberty
brotherhood
freedom
gifts
satisfaction

Exercise 2

families
organization
membership
ideologies
functions
marriage
cultures
members
perspectives
conflict
idea
family
love
joy
people
satisfaction
families
assumption
aspects
(family) life
families
love
hate
tenderness
spite
violence
product
tensions
stresses
Children
world
temperaments
characteristics
Children
agents

Exercise 3

family
framework
society
fount
creativeness
survival
knowledge
(human) beings
desires
selfishness
aggression
competition
self-control
capacity
love
Civilization
self-control
prohibitions
generosity
orderliness
(family) life

construction
knowledge
world

CONCRETE NOUNS

Exercise 1	Exercise 2	Exercise 3
wind	(Hebrew)literature	Bible
trees	(ancient) literature	(sacred) book
picnic	(folk) songs	(Old Testament) books
park	legends	books
Germs	camps	library
eyes	(village) gatherings	writings
sun	(tribal) bards	sketches
snowstorm	poems	legends
roads	Bible	laws
boys	songs	utterances
(football) game	fragments	visions
shoes	poems	poems
room		poetry
sound		fiction
music		poem
purse		
trunk		
paint		

COLLECTIVE NOUNS

Exercise 1	Exercise 2	Exercise 3
school	writings	document
company	Pentateuch	scholars
army	Scientists	documents
circus	Pentateuch	narratives
town	writers	documents
people	writers	Bible
news	writings	writings
vitamins	documents	laws
crop	Kingdoms	customs
family		
neighborhood		
crowd		
team		
crew		

COMPOUND NOUNS

Exercise 1
cupful
Secretary-General
United Nations
pancakes
maple syrup
brother-in-law
motorboat
"have-nots"
Native Americans
businessmen
Chamber of Commerce
passer-by
President-elect
playground
schoolgirls
schoolboys

Exercise 2
mankind's
English-speaking
story-tellers
newspapers
world language

Exercise 3
countrymen
safe-conduct
safeguard
Queen Mary
Lincoln Memorial

GENDER

Exercise 1
people - C
homes - N
summertime - N
vacations - N
times - N
fun - N
oil - N
car - N
industry - N
town - N
injuries - N
accident - N
doctor - C

Exercise 1 (cont.)
treatments - N
child - C
clown - C
people - C
pasture - N
cows - F
bull - M
girls - F
boys - M
outside - N
recess - N
snake - C

Exercise 2
mother-in-law (sister-in-law)
hens (roosters)
hostess
Princess
woman

PERSON
Dad - 2
soup - 3
Mary - 2
hunter - 1
Mother - 2

NUMBER
children - P
yard - S
signs - P
crossings - P
handwriting - S

NUMBER (cont.)
maps - P
secretaries - P
stack - S
letters - P
nations - P

John - 2
car - 3
Abraham Lincoln - 3
Mike - 3
Lord - 1

way - S
store - S
dimes - P
bell - S
homework - S

treaty - S
people - P
ability - S
things - P
computer - S

REVIEW OF FOUNDATION I

Exercise 1
Rosebud - Compound
Alaska - Proper
Americans - Collective
Safety - Abstract
Homework - Compound
Women - Collective
Ann - Proper
Team - Collective
Football - Compound
Cow - Common
Skill - Common
Man - Common

Exercise 2
day - Common
people - Common
Lincoln Memorial - Proper
Washington - Proper
monument - Common
Henry Bacon - Proper
Memorial Day - Proper
West Potomac Park - Proper
Lincoln Memorial - Proper
hall - Common
statue - Common
Abraham Lincoln - Proper
figure - Common
blocks - Common
marble - Common
Daniel Chester French - Pro
sculptor - Common
armchair - Common
meditation - Common
wall - Common
passage - Common
Inaugural Address - Proper
Lincoln - Proper
wall - Common
Gettysburg Address -Proper

Exercise 3
Friends - Collective
Romans - Proper
Countrymen - Collective
ears - Concrete
Caesar - Proper
schemes - Common
mice - Collective
men - Collective
heart - Concrete
rainbow - Concrete
sky - Concrete
thing - Common
beauty - Abstract
joy - Abstract
year - Common
kingdom - Concrete
sea - Concrete
maiden - Concrete
Annebel Lee - Proper
wagon - Concrete
star - Concrete
night - Concrete
music - Concrete
cares - Abstract
day - Concrete
tents - Concrete
Arabs - Proper
paths - Common
glory - Abstract
grave - Concrete
object - Abstract
avocation - Abstract
vocation - Abstract

quality - Abstract
mercy - Abstract
rain - Concrete
heaven - Common
place - Common

ENGLISH FOUNDATIONS

FOUNDATION II

PRONOUNS

A **PRONOUN** is a word that is used to take the place of a noun. **PRO** means <u>for</u> or <u>stand for</u>.

Example: Judy read the novel and returned *it* to the library.

Example: The members of the wedding party bought *themselves* matching dresses.

Example: "Students," the teacher said, "*You* should keep your notes in a folder."

The noun for which the pronoun is used is called the **ANTECEDENT**. This noun is not always stated although it is understood.

Example: Joseph told *his* mother that *he* would be late for supper.

Example: Jane, did *you* do *your* homework?

Example: *You* can't sleep well with the lights on.

EXERCISE. <u>Underline</u> the <u>pronouns</u> in the following sentences. Above each pronoun, <u>write</u> the <u>noun</u> or <u>nouns</u> to which the pronoun refers. Write <u>U</u> if noun is not stated. (Possible Score: 32)

1. The marksman fired at the distant target until he finally hit it.

2. "I know the answer, but I can't think of it right now," exclaimed the contestant.

3. "Sarah, have you bought the refreshments for the party tonight?"

4. "Listen to me," pleaded Josephine.

5. When the children found the abandoned kittens, they carried them home.

6. The parade was an exciting sight as it moved down Main Street.

7. College students are given ten minutes to get to their next class.

8. Eighty-five percent of people surveyed considered themselves to be above average.

9. John and Jerry went fishing. They caught several sunfish.

10. You never know when you will need the information you learn in school.

Answers are on page 41. Subtract one point for each incorrect answer. *Your Score:* _____

A pronoun generally agrees with its antecedent in **GENDER** (male, female, neuter, common), **PERSON** (first, second, third), and **NUMBER** (singular or plural).

>Example: My mother is going to her ceramics class today. (**HER** agrees with the antecedent <u>mother</u>. It is female, third person, singular.

>Example: I had fun with John. I want to go with him again. (**HIM** agrees with the antecedent <u>John</u>. It is male, third person, singular.

Like nouns, pronouns also differ from each other according to gender, person, and number.

>Example: <u>I</u> told <u>you</u> to let go of <u>her</u>. (<u>I</u> is first person (the person speaking), singular number, and masculine or feminine, depending on who is speaking. <u>You</u> is second person (the person spoken to), singular or plural, depending on how many there are, and masculine or feminine, since the gender is not mentioned. <u>Her</u> is third person (the person spoken about), singular, and feminine.)

>Example: Are <u>you</u> going to the dance with <u>them</u>? (<u>You</u> is second person, masculine or feminine, and singular or plural. <u>Them</u> is third person, masculine or feminine, and plural.

Pronouns are called **PERSONAL** when they refer to a person or persons. Simple personal pronouns include *I, me, you, (which is the same in both singular and plural; you can tell from the sentence which it I)s, he ,him, she, it, we, us they, and them.*

EXERCISE 1. <u>Underline </u>the personal pronoun or pronouns in the following sentences. Above each, <u>put a **1**</u> if it is first person, 2 if it is second person, or 3 if it is third person. (Possible Score: 18)

1.   I want to tell you about a strange experience I had.

2.   I have a friend, Bill Glenn, who was leading a group of scientists through Australia.

3.   After traveling for hours through wilderness, we in the group wanted to make camp, but he insisted that we continue on.

4.   Finally, we decided to travel for just one more hour.

5.   Soon, we were rewarded for the trip. Before long, several strange-looking people had collected in a clearing.

Answers on page 41. Subtract one point for each incorrect answer. *Your Score:* _____

EXERCISE 2. <u>Continue as above</u>. (Possible Score: 16)

1. The scientists watched them from a distance. We dared not speak a word.

2. The women in the group dug up roots with stones. They prepared meat with crude implements.

3. The scientists were watching the aborigines. They are still living as people did during the Stone Age.

4. Although we of the Australian tribes have become civilized, they continue to follow primitive ways.

5. We marveled that they could be living so primitive an existence in the twentieth century.

Answers are on page 41. Subtract one point for each incorrect answer. *Your Score:* _____

APPLICATION. Write 5 sentences using Personal pronouns. Underline the Personal pronoun or pronouns in each sentence.

1._____

2._____

3._____

4._____

5._____

A **RELATIVE PRONOUN** is not only a pronoun but is also a connecting word. It connects a ependent clause, of which it is a part, with a noun or pronoun in another clause. The noun or pronoun to which the relative pronoun points back is called the **ANTECEDENT**.

> Example: I am the man <u>who</u> applied for the job. (The relative pronoun WHO refers back to the noun <u>man</u>.)

> Example: Albert Einstein was a scientist of the 20th. Century <u>whose</u> theories are still considered valid. (The relative pronoun WHOSE refers back to the noun <u>Albert Einstein</u>.

The relative pronouns are **WHO, WHOM, WHOSE, WHICH, WHAT,** and **THAT**. **WHAT** has no antecedent.

COMPOUND RELATIVE PRONOUNS are formed by adding -ever or -soever- to who, whose, whom, what, and which.

>Example: I can give a gift to <u>whomever</u> I wish.

>Example: <u>Whoever</u> wants to go shopping with me should be ready in twenty minutes.

WHATEVER, WHATSOEVER, WHOEVER, and **WHOSOEVER** have no antecedent.

When you use relative pronouns, generally use **WHO** or **WHOM** when you refer to persons; **WHICH** when you refer to animals and things; and **THAT** when you refer to persons, animals, places, or things.

>Example: This is the man who offered to pick up your groceries for you.

>Example: There are many things that are considered mysteries.

EXERCISE 1. <u>Underline</u> the <u>relative pronoun</u> in the following sentences. <u>Above</u> the pronoun, <u>write</u> its <u>antecedent</u>. If there is no antecedent, write <u>none</u>. (Possible Score: 20)

1.   Johnny is the new boy in school about whom I was telling you.

2.   This is the day that the Lord has made.

3.   She is a woman whose qualities are greatly admired.

4.   This is the man whose car was reported stolen.

5.   You can never tell what he is going to do next.

6.   There is a saying which goes like this: a stitch in time saves nine.

7.   The man whom you saw yesterday was my father.

8.   Stop anyone who tries to come through this gate.

9.   You can do whatever you want.

10.   Whatsoever you do to the least of my brothers you do to me.

Answers are on page 41. Subtract one point for each incorrect score. *Your Score:* _____

EXERCISE 2. Underline the relative pronoun in the following sentences. Above the pronoun, write its antecedent. If there is no antecedent, write none. (Possible Score: 20)

1.   Words that mean the opposite of another word are called antonyms.

2.   One sport that is becoming very popular in the mountains is hang gliding.

3.   Whoever wants to come to the dance must have a date.

4.   You can do whatever you want as long as it is not illegal or immoral.

5.   A $1,000 prize will be awarded to the student who writes the best essay.

6.   The bride invited everyone whom she knew to her wedding.

7.   In her journal, Susie recorded everything that she did and thought.

8.   The fugitive whom the police had been seeking for several years was finally arrested.

9.   The singer who is scheduled to lead off the program has arrived.

10.   In this art class you can paint whatever you want.

Answers are on page 41. Subtract one point for each incorrect answer. *Your Score:* _____

APPLICATION. Write 5 sentences using relative pronouns. Underline the relative pronoun in each sentence.

1 _____

2. _____

3. _____

4. _____

5. _____

POSSESSIVE PRONOUNS are personal pronouns that show they belong to something or someone (ownership). Make sure the possessive pronoun agrees with its antecedent in number.

> Example: Each boy should make <u>his</u> own model.

> Example: All of the girls are responsible for <u>their</u> chores before they go to school.

The pronouns **MY, OUR, HER, THEIR,** and **YOUR** always go <u>before</u> the noun whose ownership they show.

> Example: Who is that driving <u>my</u> car?

> Example: Welcome to <u>our</u> new home.

The pronouns **MINE, OURS, HERS, THEIRS,** and **YOURS** go <u>after</u> the noun to which they refer. They can also stand alone.

> Example: The boat over there is <u>mine</u>. (<u>Mine</u> refers back to <u>boat</u>.)

> Example: Whose house is that? <u>Ours</u>. (<u>Ours</u> refers back to <u>house</u> but stands alone.)

The pronouns **HIS** and **ITS** can be used either way.

> Example: Our cat is not eating <u>its</u> food. (<u>Its</u> refers back to <u>cat</u>.)

> Example: The dog thought that the bone was <u>its</u>. <u>Its</u> refers back to the <u>dog</u>.)

> Example: The artist stood back and admired <u>his</u> handiwork.

> Example: Whose pizza is this that was left on the counter? <u>His</u>.

EXERCISE 1. <u>Underline</u> the <u>possessive pronoun</u> or <u>pronouns</u> in the following sentences. (Possible Score: 12)

1.   The navy fought on the high seas to protect our liberties.

2.   We tend to bury memories of our injuries.

3.   Which one of these coats is yours?

4.   Who put the strawberries in my grocery bag?

5. Lucy made a big fuss over her beauty.

6. How much of this money is ours, and how much is theirs?

7. I am their new friendly and reliable bus driver.

8. Your gloves are all torn up.

9. Some of these cupcakes are mine, and some are hers.

10. Did someone break into your house last night?

Answers are on page 41. Subtract one point for each incorrect answer. *Your Score:* _____

EXERCISE 2. Underline the possessive pronoun or pronouns in the following sentences. (Possible Score: 5)

1. Many centuries ago, people carried clubs for their defense when they went anywhere.

2. While a peasant was visiting a priest for confession, he would stand his club at the end of the cloister.

3. Eventually, the clubs came to represent their sins.

4. After the peasants had finished their confessions, they rolled large stones at the clubs.

5. If one knocked over his club, he was leading a good life. Thus began bowling.

Answers are on page 41. Subtract one point for each incorrect answer. *Your Score:* _____

APPLICATION. Write 5 sentences using possessive pronouns. Underline the possessive pronoun or pronouns in each sentence.

1._____

2._____

3._____

4._____

5._____

When the pronouns **WHO, WHOM, WHOSE, WHICH,** and **WHAT** are used in asking questions, they are called **INTERROGATIVE PRONOUNS**.

EXERCISE 1. Underline the interrogative pronoun in the following sentences. (Possible Score: 5)

1.   Whose car just sped away?

2.   Who is going to go to the store for me?

3.   Which of these dresses should I wear today?

4.   Whom shall I invite to dinner tonight?

5.   What are you going to do after school?

Answers are on page 41. Subtract one point for each incorrect answer. *Your Score:* _____

APPLICATION. Write 5 sentences using each of the interrogative pronouns above.

1._____

2._____

3._____

4._____

5._____

Pronouns are called **INDEFINITE** when it is not clear to what person, place, or thing they refer.

The following indefinite pronouns are singular and take singular verbs: **EACH, EITHER, NEITHER, ONE, EVERYONE, EVERYBODY, NO ONE, NOBODY, ANYONE, ANYBODY, SOMEONE,** and **SOMEBODY**.

Example: Nobody told me that I was not supposed to eat the cake.

Example: Will someone please tell me where I can get some gas?

The indefinite pronouns **BOTH, FEW, OTHERS, SEVERAL,** and **MANY** are plural and take plural verbs.

> Example: <u>Few</u> of the guests arrived at the appointed time.

> Example: <u>Several</u> of the states have Indian names.

> Example: <u>Some</u> people succeed through the use of their physical skills. <u>Others</u> succeed through their intellectual abilities.

The indefinite pronouns **SOME, ANY, NONE, ALL,** and **MOST** may be either singular or plural.

> Example: <u>Some</u> birds have already gone south for the winter.

> Example: <u>Some</u> of the glitter has disappeared.

Indefinite pronouns always **STAND ALONE**. If one of these words is found with a noun to which it clearly refers, it is no longer a pronoun but an **ADJECTIVE**.

> Example: <u>Each</u> person in this class will speak once. (<u>Each</u> clearly refers to person, so is an adjective.)

> Example: <u>Anyone</u> who wants to go swimming can do so after 10 a.m. (<u>Anyone</u> stands alone, so is a pronoun.)

EXERCISE 1. <u>Underline</u> the <u>indefinite pronoun</u> or <u>pronouns</u> in the following sentences. <u>Put</u> an <u>**S**</u> above it if it is <u>singular</u> in number, and <u>**P**</u> if it is plural in number. (Possible Score: 26)

1. Almost everyone can sing the National Anthem.

2. "Nobody knows the trouble I've seen."

3. Neither of us was present when they presented the awards.

4. Few ever develop the potential they have within themselves.

5. I am going to ask somebody to go with me.

6. Many are called, but few are chosen.

7. Many came to the party, but not everyone enjoyed it.

8. Each of us is allowed to make mistakes so we can learn from them.

9. You can both go to the movies if you have enough money.

10. All of the employees were invited to the Christmas Party, but several chose not to attend.

Answers are on page 42. Subtract one point for each incorrect answer. *Your Score:* ____

EXERCISE 2. Underline the indefinite pronoun or pronouns in the following sentences. Then, underline the correct verb in the parentheses). Possible score:10)

1. All of the entries (is, are) on display.

2. Each of the entries (has, have) a special characteristic.

3. Someone in this group (is, are) not paying attention.

4. Some of the artists in this contest (use, uses) different techniques.

5. Many of them (work, works) with sawdust, nails, and sand.

Answers are on page 42. Subtract one point for each incorrect answer. *Your Score:* ____

EXERCISE 3. Continue as above. (Possible Score: 10)

1. Both of the rock concerts (look, looks) exciting.

2. Everyone in the first two rows (win, wins) a special prize.

3. No one except the dignitaries (is, are) allowed on the stage.

4. Most of the road (has, have) been closed for two months now.

5. (Does, do) either of the stores stay open on Sundays?

Answers are on page 42. Subtract one point for each incorrect answer. *Your Score:* ____

APPLICATION. Write 10 sentences using indefinite pronouns. Put an **S** above those that are singular, and a **P** above those that are plural.

1._____

2._____

3._____

4._____

5._____

REVIEW OF FOUNDATION II

EXERCISE 1. Underline each pronoun in the following sentences. Above it, put **PER** if it is personal, **REL** if it is relative, **POS** if it is possessive, **INT** if it is interrogative, or **IND** if it is indefinite. (Possible Score: 50)

1.   All of us hoped to win the skating contest.

2.   Almost everyone tends to overestimate the intelligence of the horse.

3.   Who would not like to take a gondola ride through one of the canals of Venice?

4.   The bitter Scrooge would not share his wealth with anyone.

5.   We planned a street dance to celebrate the victory of our football team.

6.   When the mountain called the proud little squirrel a weakling, the squirrel replied,

        "If I cannot carry forests on my back, neither can you crack a nut."

7.   When someone visits Rome, he or she sees many of the wonders of ancient times.

8.   "These are people who really need our help," explained our guide.

9.   Each of the boys found that he was a better swimmer than he thought.

10.   Several of them drew pictures of the people whom they had seen on the beach.

Answers are on page 42. Subtract one point for each incorrect answer. *Your Score:* ____

EXERCISE 2. Same as above. (Possible Score: 98)

1.   What am I going to do with you when he goes to work?

2. He doesn't know what to do while his brothers and sisters are at school.

3. He is the man whose dog I walk early in the morning while everybody else is asleep.

4. Anyone who wants to go with us must bring his or her own lunch.

5. Several wanted to go to the concert, but they had trouble getting their schedules changed, which complicated the situation.

6. Who said she had given them all the information they needed to make their own decisions?

7. None of us likes to tell someone that he or she needs to correct patterns of behavior that are causing them problems.

8. What needs to happen is for each of us to take responsibility for his or her actions and to bring them into line with the moral code of our society.

9. You and I can make decisions which can make us happier than we thought possible.

10. Whomever you wish to invite to your party is fine with me. The decision is entirely yours.

Answers are on page 42. Subtract one point for each incorrect answer. *Your Score:* _____

ANSWERS TO FOUNDATION II

ANTECEDENT	PERSONAL	PERSONAL (cont.)
Exercise 1	**Exercise 1**	**Exercise 2**
he - marksman	I - 1	them - 3
it - target	you - 2	we - 1
I - u	I - 1	they - 3
I - u	I- 1	they - 3

it - answer   we- 1   we - 1
you - Sarah   he - 3   they - 3
me - Josephine   we - 1   we - 1
they - children   we - 1   they - 3
them - kittens   we - 1
it - parade
their - class
themselves - people
they - John and Jerry
you - u
you - u
you - u

RELATIVE PRONOUNS

Exercise 1.   **Exercise 2.**

whom - Johnny   that - words
that - day   that - sport
whose - woman   whoever - none
whose - man   whatever - none
what - none   who - student
which - saying   whom - everyone
whom - man   that - everything
who - anyone   whom - fugitive
whatever - none   who - singer
whatsoever - none   whatever - none

POSSESSIVE PRONOUNS

INTERROGATIVE

Exercise 1   **Exercise 2**   **Exercise 1**

our   their   whose
our   his   who
yours   their   which
my   their   whom
her   his   what
ours
theirs
their
your
mine
hers
your

INDEFINITE PRONOUNS

Exercise 1
everyone - S
nobody - S
neither - S
few - P
somebody - S
many - P
few - P
many - P
everyone - S
each - S
both - P
all - p
several - p

Exercise 2
all - are
each - has
someone - is
many - work

Exercise 3
both - look
everyone - wins
no one - is
most - has

REVIEW OF FOUNDATION II

Exercise 1
all - ind
us - per
everyone - ind
who - int
one - ind
his - pos
anyone - ind
we - per
our - pos
I - per
my - pos
you - per
someone - ind
he - per
she - per
many - ind
who - rel
our - pos
each - ind
he - per
he - per
several - ind
them - per

Exercise 2
what - int
I - per
you -per
he - per
he - per
what - rel
his - pos
he - per
whose - rel
I - per
everybody - ind
anyone - ind
who - rel
us - per
his - pos
her - pos
several - ind
they - per
their - pos
which - rel
who - int
she - per
them - per

Exercise 2 (cont.)
none - ind
us - per
someone - per
that - rel
he - per
she - per
that - rel
them - per
what - rel
each - ind
his - pos
her - pos
them - per
our - pos
you - per
I - per
which - rel
us - per
we - per
whomever - ind
you - per
your - pos
me - per

whom - rel   they - per   yours - pos
they - per   their - pos

ENGLISH FOUNDATIONS

FOUNDATION III

ADJECTIVES

An **ADJECTIVE** is a word that **TELLS SOMETHING ABOUT** a noun or pronoun.

Some adjectives answer the questions **WHAT KIND** or **WHICH ONE**?

> Example: I drive a <u>blue</u> and <u>white</u> sportscar.

> Example: Isn't this a <u>beautiful</u> day?

> Example: The <u>other</u> day I went to the beauty parlor.

Some adjectives answer the questions **HOW MANY** or **HOW MUCH**?

> Example: There were <u>twenty-five</u> people at the party.

> Example: <u>Several</u> divers were needed to rescue the drowning swimmer.

> Example: I have only <u>two gallons</u> of gas to get home on.

Some adjectives **POINT TO** something that is near or close by. There are only four of this kind: **THIS, THAT, THESE,** and **THOSE.** These four adjectives are called **DEMONSTRATIVE** adjectives.

THIS and **THAT** point to only one thing, so they refer to *singular* nouns only.

> Example: I want <u>that</u> piece of candy.

> Example: I am satisfied with <u>this</u> prize.

THESE and **THOSE** point to more than one thing, so they refer to *plural* nouns only.

> Example: I would like <u>those</u> shirts dry-cleaned.

> Example: <u>These</u> boxes are too heavy for me to carry.

Some adjectives come from a **PROPER NOUN.**

> Example: The <u>American</u> Indians were here long before the white man. (America is a proper noun.)

> Example: We will never forget the <u>Vietnamese</u> War. (Vietnam is a proper noun.)

The articles **A, AN,** and **THE** are also adjectives.

Example: I would like <u>a</u> glass of water.

Example: Would you walk <u>the</u> dog before supper?

EXERCISE 1. <u>Underline</u> each <u>adjective</u> in the following sentences. <u>Above</u> it put **PT** if it <u>points to</u> something near or close by, **WK** if it answers <u>what kind</u> or <u>which one</u>, **HM** if it answers <u>how many</u> or <u>how much</u>, **A** if it is an <u>article</u>, and **P** if it comes from a <u>proper noun</u>. (Possible Score: 62)

1.   There are many navies in the world today.

2.   In this contest, you an win a year's supply of Idaho potatoes.

3.   The sign said, "No Trespassing on this private property."

4.   Look at that beautiful horse!

5.   I lost twenty-five pounds since November.

6.   These bananas are yellow and those apples are green.

7.   The frisky puppy played in the tall, green grass.

8.   This year we are going to the Hawaiian Islands..

9.   Two heads bumped while bobbing for apples in the babbling brook.

10.   My Siamese cat is a friendly and faithful feline.

Answers are on page 48. Subtract one point for each incorrect answer. *Your Score:* _____

EXERCISE 2. <u>Underline</u> the adjectives in the following sentences. Then, <u>draw an arrow</u> from the adjective to the noun it modifies. Do not underline the articles *a, an,* and *the*. (Possible Score: 17)

1.   A large evergreen tree landed in the middle of the mobile home.

2.   The blazing sun beat down on the migrant workers.

3.   Many famous writers are buried in Westminster Abbey.

4.   The official guides at the United Nations can speak many different languages.

5.   The charming elderly couple celebrated their fiftieth wedding anniversary by performing an elegant waltz.

Answers are on page 48. Subtract one point for each incorrect answer. *Your Score:* _____

APPLICATION. Write 10 sentences using different kinds of adjectives. <u>Underline</u> each adjective, and <u>above each </u>one put **PT, HM, WK, A,** or **P** as in Exercise 1.

1._____

2._____

3._____

4._____

5._____

6._____

7._____

8._____

9._____

10._____

REVIEW OF FOUNDATION III

<u>Underline all adjectives</u> in the paragraph below. <u>Above each</u> adjective, put **PT**, **WK**, **HM**, **P** or **A** as above. (Possible Score: 48)

Pigs are stout. They have a heavy body and coarse, bristly hair. The head and short, thick neck extend in a straight line from the body. There are several kinds of pigs. These ten over here are Berkshire pigs. Those five over there are called Spotted Poland pigs. Pigs weigh about two pounds at birth and usually double their weight in just a few days. When they are fully grown, they weigh almost a thousand pounds.

Answers are on page 48. Subtract one point for each incorrect answer. *Your Score:* _____

ANSWERS TO FOUNDATION III

Exercise 1.
Many - HM
The - A
This - PT
A - A
Year's - HM
Idaho - P
The - A
This - PT
Private - WK
That - PT
Beautiful - WK
Twenty-five - HM
These - PT
Yellow - WK
Those - PT
Green - WK
The - A
Frisky - WK
Poland - P
The - A
Tall - WK
Green - WK
This - WK
The - A
Hawaiian - P
HM
Two - HM
The - A
Babbling - WK
Siamese - P
A - A
Friendly - WK
Faithful - WK

Exercise 2.
large - tree
evergreen - tree
mobile - home
blazing - sun
migrant - workers
many - writers
famous - writers
Westminster - Abbey
official - guides
United - Nations
many - languages
different - languages
charming - couple
elderly - couple
fiftieth - anniversary
wedding - anniversary
elegant - waltz

Review
Stout - WK
A - A
Heavy - WK
Coarse - WK
Bristly - WK
The - A
Short - WK
Thick - WK
A - A
Straight - WK
The - A
Several - HM
These - PT
Ten - HM
Berkshire - P
Those - PT
Five - HM
Spotted

Two - HM
A - A
Few - HM
Grown - WK
A - A
Thousand -

ENGLISH FOUNDATIONS

FOUNDATION IV

SUBJECTS

The **SUBJECT** of a sentence is the person or thing (noun or pronoun) that is **DOING** or **BEING** something. It always answers the question **WHO**? or **WHAT**?

A **SIMPLE SUBJECT** is a noun or pronoun *only*, without any words that tell about it. It may have more than one word, however.

Example: The apple fell out of the tree.

Example: Niagara Falls is a very nice place to visit.

EXERCISE 1. Underline the simple subject in the following sentences. (Possible Score: 10)

1. Peanut butter sticks to the roof of my mouth.

2. John went to the movie this afternoon.

3. Are you going to the play tonight?

4. We went to the circus last Saturday.

5. James Whitcomb Riley was a great American poet.

6. When do we get to go swimming?

7. Anyone can climb that tree with a little effort.

8. Washington, D.C. is the capital of the United States.

9. These are my favorite hunting rifles.

10. Sharon's birthday party was last Monday.

Answers are on page 54. Subtract one point for each incorrect answer. *Your Score:* ____

EXERCISE 2. Underline the simple subject in the following sentences. (Possible Score: 5)

1. The people of Israel form a part of the Semitic branch of the Caucasian race.

2. Their language, Hebrew, belongs to the Western group of Semitic languages.

3. Cradled in the great Arabian desert, they migrated to Palestine about 1400-1200 B.C.

4. They established a nation which endured until overthrown by the Romans in 70 A.D.

5. Since, then, Israel has been scattered throughout the world.

Answers are on page 54. Subtract one point for each incorrect answer. *Your Score:* ____

APPLICATION. Write 5 sentences using a simple subject and underline the simple subject in each sentence.

1._____

2._____

3._____

4._____

5._____

A **COMPOUND SUBJECT** is made up of two or more simple subjects that are doing the same thing.

> Example: My mom and dad went to the dance.

> Example: Mary, Jane, and Sally went to school together.

EXERCISE. Underline the compound subjects in the following sentences. (Possible Score: 10)

1. Cats and dogs are supposed to be natural enemies.

2. My mother and I wear the same size clothes.

3. Red, white, and blue are the colors of our National Flag.

4. Mike, Anne, and Susie contributed sentences to this book.

5. Math and Science are not my favorite subjects.

6. Susan and I had a date last night.

7. The cat and the dog wrestled playfully on the ground.

8. Tarzan and Jane swung from tree to tree.

9. John and Bobby Kennedy were both assassinated.

10. Mark, Sally, Jenny, Terry, and Bob had a picnic together.

Answers are on page 54. Subtract one point for each incorrect answer. *Your Score:* ____

APPLICATION. Write 5 sentences using compound subjects.

1._____

2._____

3._____

4._____

5._____

A **COMPLETE SUBJECT** is the subject along with all the words that tell about it.

Example: <u>Whoever wants to go to the Dairy Queen</u> should get into the car. (The simple subject is <u>whoever</u>. All the other words are necessary to describe the "whoevers" that should get into the car.)

Example: <u>The green and yellow submarine</u> sank to the bottom of the lake. (The simple subject is <u>submarine</u>. All the words that talk about it go with the simple subject to make a *complete* subject.

EXERCISE 1. <u>Underline</u> the <u>complete subject</u> in the following sentences. (Possible Score: 10)

1. The little bird sang merrily.

2. The man at the organ played continuously for one hour.

3. Those who are the strongest should help the weakest.

4.   The unexpected surprise excited the children.

5.   The point of what I am saying is not being understood.

6.   What you think about yourself affects what you will become.

7.   *"The Taming Of The Shrew"* was a play by William Shakespeare.

8.   The President of the United States signed a peace treaty with Russia.

9.   The news announcement came when I least expected it.

10.   Summer vacations pass very quickly.

Answers are on page 55. Subtract one point for each incorrect answer. *Your Score:* _____

EXERCISE 2. Underline the complete subject in the following sentences. (Possible Score: 5)

1.   A thick, gray fog settled in over the trees in the woods behind us.

2.   Many fighter jets were sent into the battle to support the troops.

3.   The emergency personnel with the food had to get through quickly.

4.   Pilots of our jet fighters must have a great deal of experience.

5.   The airline pilot taxied slowly down the taxiway to the runway.

Answers are on page 55. Subtract one point for each incorrect answer. *Your Score:* _____

APPLICATION. Write 5 sentences and underline the complete subject in each one.

1._____

2._____

3._____

4._____

5._____

REVIEW OF FOUNDATION IV

In the sentences below, underline the simple subject with one line, the compound subject with two lines, and the complete subject with three lines. (Possible Score: 23)

1.   Everyone in class watched the play.

2.   Anne and Maureen are girl scouts.

3.   The house in the middle of the block is for sale.

4.   The dining room was filled with people.

5.   Those who wish to go to Disney World should sign up soon.

6.   Are Aunt Jane and Uncle Bob coming for dinner?

7.   The oil in our car keeps leaking.

8.   The players and their coaches are doing their best.

9.   The black and white kite flew the highest.

10.   Several of those in the choir came down with sore throats.

Answers are on page 55. Subtract one point for each incorrect answer. *Your Score:* _____

ANSWERS TO FOUNDATION IV

SIMPLE SUBJECTS

Exercise 1	**Exercise 2**
Peanut butter	people
John	language
you	they
We	They
James Whitcomb Riley	Israel
we	
Anyone	
Washington, D.C.	
These	

COMPOUND SUBJECTS

Exercise
Cats and dogs
mother and I
Red, white, and blue
Mike, Anne, and Susie
Math and Science
Susan and I
the cat and the dog
Tarzan and Jane
John and Bobby Kennedy

party

Mark, Sally, Jenny, Terry, and Bob

COMPLETE SUBJECTS

Exercise 1
The little bird
The man at the organ
Those who are the strongest

The unexpected surprise
The point of what I am saying
What you think about yourself
"The Taming Of The Shrew"
The President of the United States
The news announcement
Summer vacations

Exercise 2
A thick, gray fog
Many fighter jets
The emergency personnel
with the food
Pilots of our jet fighters
The airline pilot

REVIEW OF FOUNDATION IV

Everyone in the class

_____
_____
_____

Anne and Maureen

_____
_____
_____
_____

The house in the middle of the block

_____
_____
_____

The dining room

_____
_____
_____

Aunt Jane and Uncle Bob

_____
_____
_____
_____

The oil in our car

_____
_____
_____

The players and their coach

_____
_____
_____
_____

The black and white kite

_____
_____
_____

Those who wish to go to Disney World

_____

_____

_____

Several of those in the choir

_____

_____

_____

FOUNDATION V

VERBS

VERBS are words that tell you what is going on, or that link one word with another. They express action, being, or state of being.

Example: Johnny <u>rides</u> his bike to school. (Action)

Example: Sally <u>is</u> a Brownie Scout. (Being)

Example: I <u>was</u> happy to receive my gift. (State of being)

The **SIMPLE VERB** is the verb *only*, without any words that tell about it. The simple verb will be more than one word when it includes all of its helpers.

Example: The children <u>raced</u> each other.

Example: Who <u>will be tending</u> the store tonight?

When a simple verb is made up of several words, as in the second example, it is called a **VERB PHRASE**. The **LAST** word in the phrase is called the **MAIN VERB**. The other words in the phrase are called **HELPING VERBS**.

Verbs used as helping verbs are the following:

am	been	has	do	shall	may
are	is	have	does	will	might
be	were	had	did	should	can
being	was		must	would	could

Sometimes more than one of these are used together to help the main verb.

Example: John <u>should have been chosen</u> for the part in the play.

Example: I <u>might be going</u> to the prom.

Look carefully for *any* and *all* helping verbs as well as the main verb.

Sometimes the helping verbs are used by themselves.

Example: I <u>am</u> glad that today is Friday.

Example: I <u>will be</u> available for work next Monday.

EXERCISE 1. <u>Underline</u> the <u>simple verb</u> or <u>verbs</u> in the following sentences. (Possible Score: 13)

1.   Donald Shapiro and Howard Dandrige are cousins.

2.   Tomorrow at this time we will be members of the club.

3.   The girls are walking home from school today.

4.   Mary could have been here on time.

5.   Anne said that the songs in the book are hymns.

6.   "What colors of dye do we have?" asked Jane.

7.   When will we be leaving on our trip?

8.   My car runs better when it is tuned up.

9.   Will you be going to the football game tomorrow?

10.   You must have seen that accident.

Answers are on page 63. Subtract one point for each incorrect answer. *Your Score:* ____

EXERCISE 2. <u>Underline</u> the <u>simple verb</u> or <u>verbs</u> in the following sentences. (Possible Score: 11)

1.   Alaska and Texas are two of the largest states in our country.

2.   Many people donated both books and money to the library during our fund drive.

3.   You may use either pens or pencils on this test.

4.   At one time, the twist was a very popular dance.

5.   One of you must pay the bill for the broken glass.

6.   We rested in the shade after working in the hot sun for an hour.

7.   The treasurer should present a financial report at each meeting.

8.   Have you ever listened to the *New World Symphony*?

9. A distinguished architect will be hired to design our new school building.

10. Who would have thought that the computer could have come so far in such a short time!

Answers are on page 63. Subtract one point for each incorrect answer. *Your Score:* ____

APPLICATION. Write 5 sentences using simple verbs. Underline the simple verb or verbs in your sentences.

1._____

2._____

3._____

4._____

5._____

A **COMPOUND VERB** is made up of two or more simple verbs but has only one subject.

Example: The girls ran and jumped into the swimming pool.

Example: I am and will be working until tomorrow morning.

EXERCISE. Underline the compound verb in the following sentences. (Possible Score: 21)

1. I just arrived but must leave again.

2. The entertainer sang and danced the whole evening.

3. Jerry designed and built the sports car by himself.

4. Some people don't care if they live or die.

5. I brought the beggar in and fed him.

6. Sandra cleaned her room and made her bed.

7. We buy, sell, and trade used cars.

8.   Mary went to the store but couldn't find what she was looking for.

9.   We were married in 1974 and moved to Florida.

10.   Bob and Ann bought their house in 1966 and sold it ten years later for twice as much.

Answers are on page 63. Subtract one point for each incorrect answer. *Your Score:* _____

APPLICATION. Write 5 sentences using compound verbs.

1._____

2._____

3._____

4._____

5._____

The **COMPLETE VERB** is the verb with all the other words that tell more about it. It usually comes after the subject, but it can sometimes appear at the beginning of the sentence.

> Example: The boy has tried patiently. (Patiently tells how the boy tried.)

> Example: The girl ran quickly from the room. (Quickly from the room tells more about how and where she ran.)

> Example: At the top of the tree is a bird's nest.

EXERCISE 1. Underline the complete verb in the following sentences. (Possible Score: 10)

1.   Those three dogs were barking all night.

2.   Joey can run fast.

3.   I must go to the store.

4.   From limb to limb jumped the happy squirrel.

5. Mike is out chopping wood.

6. Are you satisfied with your grades?

7. Anne is out picking berries.

8. He replied to the question.

9. We were defeated soundly.

10. Out in the shed are the hedge trimmers and the lawn mower.

Answers are on page 64. Subtract one point for each incorrect answer. *Your Score:* ____

EXERCISE 2. Underline the complete verb in the following sentences. (Possible Score: 5)

1. The basketball star signed autographs for an hour.

2. The raging flood swept through the town.

3. Many tree limbs snapped from the weight of the ice.

4. For many centuries, madness was associated with the moon.

5. There on its back was a large tortoise.

Answers are on page 64. Subtract one point for each incorrect answer. *Your Score:* ____

APPLICATION. Write 5 sentences using complete verbs. Underline the complete verbs in each sentence.

1._____

2._____

3._____

4._____

5._____

REVIEW OF FOUNDATION V

In the following sentences, underline the simple verb with one line, the compound verb with two lines, and the complete verb with three lines. (Possible Score: 22)

1.   Did someone break into your house last night?

2.   I have just noticed how quiet it is.

3.   Sandra dove off the 10 foot board and swam to the other end of the pool.

4.   I really like to paint but don't like to clean up the mess.

5.   Mike is out wading in the pool.

6.   What are you looking for?

7.   The doctor treated the child and sent her right back home.

8.   I will not be going to the baseball game.

9.   I searched everywhere but couldn't find my other shoe.

10.   Will you be starting your new job tomorrow?

Answers are on page 64. Subtract one point for each incorrect answer. *Your Score:* ____

ANSWERS TO FOUNDATION V

SIMPLE VERBS   **COMPOUND VERBS**

Exercise 1	**Exercise 2**	**Exercise**
are	are	arrived and must leave
will be	donated	sang and danced
are walking	may use	designed and built
could have been	was	live or die
said	must pay	brought and fed
are	rested	cleaned and made
do have	should present	buy, sell, and trade
asked	have listened	went but couldn't find
will be leaving	will be hired	were and moved
runs	would have thought	bought and sold

is   could have come
will be going
must have seen

COMPLETE VERBS

Exercise 1   **Exercise 2**
were barking all night   signed autographs for an hour
can run fast   swept through the town
must go to the store   snapped from the weight of
the ice
from limb to limb jumped   was associated with the moon
is out chopping wood   there on its back was
are satisfied with your grades
is out picking berries
replied to the question
were defeated soundly
out in the shed are

REVIEW OF FOUNDATION V

<u>Did break</u> into your house last night?

_____
_____
_____

<u>Have noticed</u> how quiet it is

_____
_____
_____

<u>Dove</u> off the 10 foot board and <u>swam</u> to the other end of the pool
____   ____
_____
_____
_____

<u>Like</u> to paint but <u>don't like</u> to clean up the mess
____   _____
_____
_____
_____

Is out wading in the pool

_____

_____

_____

Are looking for

_____

_____

_____

Treated the child and sent her right back home

_____   _____

_____

_____

_____

Will not be going to the baseball game

_____

_____

_____

Searched everywhere but couldn't find my other shoe

_____   _____

_____

_____

_____

Will be starting your new job tomorrow

_____

_____

_____

ENGLISH FOUNDATIONS

FOUNDATION VI

SUBJECT-VERB AGREEMENT

SINGULAR VERBS are used when the subject is singular number (only one). The number of the subject is not changes by a prepositional phrase following the subject.

Example: My cat <u>likes</u> to eat a lot. (Cat is singular).

Example: The crowd in the halls is unusually large.

Singular verbs are used when singular subjects are joined by **OR** or **NOR**.

Example: Neither sleet nor hail <u>keeps</u> the mail carrier from his rounds. (<u>Sleet</u> and <u>hail</u> are both singular).

Example: Either Jenny or Peter <u>is helping</u> me after school. (<u>Jenny</u> and <u>Peter</u> are both singular).

Singular verbs are used when the subject is **EACH, ANYONE, EVERYONE, EVERYBODY, NOBODY, SOMEBODY, SOMEONE, EITHER,** or **NEITHER**.

Example: Nobody <u>likes</u> my pancakes.

EXERCISE 1. <u>Underline</u> the <u>singular verb</u> or <u>verbs</u> in the following sentences with <u>one</u> line. <u>Underline</u> the <u>subject or subjects</u> with two lines. (Possible Score: 25)

1.   Is either Jack or Tom going with you to the mall?

2.   Somebody told me the funniest joke yesterday.

3.   The orchestra contains many instruments but sounds like one great voice.

4.   Neither of us is able to solve the puzzle.

5.   Each of you can take a turn throwing the ball.

6.   Neither rain nor sunshine excuses you from coming to work.

7.   Everyone likes to go swimming in the summertime.

8.   Richard will go to the store tomorrow and will buy himself a new shirt.

9.   The rating, not the amount, of insulation is what counts.

10.   A dollar doesn't go very far today.

Answers are on page 71. Subtract one point for each incorrect answer. *Your Score:* ____

EXERCISE 2. Underline the singular verb or verbs with one line. Underline the subject or subjects with two lines. If the subject is understood, put a U before the sentence. (Possible Score: 10)

1.   No one stays long after the performance.

2.   Never burn a candle at both ends.

3.   Whoever comes in first also wins the prize.

4.   The car came to a screeching halt.

5.   Whatever happened to honesty and integrity?

Answers are on page 71. Subtract one point for each incorrect answer. *Your Score:* ____

APPLICATION. Write 5 sentences applying each of the rules above.

1._____

2._____

3._____

4._____

5._____

PLURAL VERBS are used when the subject is plural. Generally, subjects ending in *s* are plural.

    Example: The hamburgers smell delicious.

Plural verbs are used when subjects are joined by **AND** unless such subjects form one unit.

    Example: Joe and Karen like to skate together.

    Example: Bacon and eggs is my favorite breakfast. (Here, bacon and eggs is usually thought of as one dish).

Plural verbs are used when plural subjects are joined by **OR** or **NOR**.

Example: Neither apples nor peaches taste good when they are spoiled.

EXERCISE 1. Underline the plural verb or verbs in the following sentences with one line. Underline the subject or subjects with two lines. (Possible Score: 28)

1.   Rocks and shells make beautiful craft items.

2.   Sam and Joe are warming up in the bullpen.

3.   Neither the clutch nor the brakes were working properly.

4.   The police have closed in on the scene of the robbery.

5.   Either riches or pleasures can trap someone into a life of emptiness.

6.   There are many types of people in the world.

7.   Are Sheila and Jerry going on the outing with us this Saturday?

8.   The thrills, glamour, and excitement of a large circus motivate those who are involved.

9.   Pieces of the broken up satellite fell everywhere.

10.   Neither riches nor possessions attract me.

Answers are on page 72. Subtract one point for each incorrect answer. *Your Score:* _____

EXERCISE 2. Underline the plural verb or verbs with one line. Underline the subject or subjects with two lines. (Possible Score: 12)

1.   Many maple trees in our yard are in bloom.

2.   Scientists work many hours trying to come up with a cure.

3.   Some students have to work very hard to maintain good grades.

4.   The chimes in the tower play hymns every noon.

5.   The French horn, the bassoon, and the oboe are wind instruments.

Answers are on page 72. Subtract one point for each incorrect answer. *Your Score:* _____

APPLICATION. Write 5 sentences applying the rules above.

1._____

2._____

3._____

4._____

5._____

When a **SINGULAR SUBJECT** and a **PLURAL SUBJECT** are joined by **OR** or **NOR**, the verb agrees with the subject closest to it.

   Example: Either Sam or his friends <u>are lying</u>.

   Example: Neither the players nor the coach <u>was</u> on time for the game.

When possible, avoid this kind of sentence by rewriting it.

   Example: Both the players and the coach were late for the game.

REVIEW OF FOUNDATION VI

EXERCISE 1. <u>Underline</u> the <u>proper verb form</u> in each of the following sentences. (Possible Score: 10)

1.   Each of these pictures (is, are) beautifully painted.

2.   A smart student (use, uses) his study time productively.

3.   (Does, do) Joe and Cathy know that you want to go with them?

4.   There (is, are) some fresh peaches in the refrigerator.

5.   Either Sam or Nancy (is going, are going) to go with you.

6.   The care of the kittens, not the milking of the cow, (is, are) my responsibility.

7.	Peaches and cream (make, makes) a delightful treat on a hot day.

8.	Everyone in our class (is going, are going) on the outing.

9.	Neither the end nor the beginning of the story (was, were) very well written.

10.	Each of us (has, have) to decide what we will do with our life.

Answers are on page 72. Subtract one point for each incorrect answer. *Your Score:* _____

EXERCISE 2. Underline the proper verb form in the following sentences. (Possible Score: 5)

1.	Either lemonade or ice tea (taste, tastes) good on a hot day.

2.	Chicken and dumplings (are, is) a favorite dish in the South.

3.	Galileo and Copernicus (was, were) famous astronomers.

4.	Last year an opera hall and a baseball stadium (was, were) built in our city.

5.	Mathematics and science (requires, require) many hours of study.

Answers are on page 72. Subtract one point for each incorrect answer. *Your Score:* _____

ANSWERS TO FOUNDATION VI

SINGULAR VERBS

Exercise 1
is going - Jack or Tom
told - somebody
contains - orchestra
is able - neither
can take - each
excuses - rain, sunshine
likes - everyone
will go - Richard
is - rating, amount
doesn't go - dollar

Exercise 2
stays - no one
burn - U (you is understood)
comes - whoever
happened - whatever

PLURAL VERBS

Exercise 1
make - rocks, shells
are warming up - Sam, Joe
were working, clutch, brakes
have closed in - police
can trap - riches, pleasures
are - there
going - Sheila, Jerry
motivate - thrills, glamour, excitement
fell - pieces
attract - riches, possessions

Exercise 2
are - trees
work - scientists
have to work - students
play - chimes
are - French horn, bassoon, oboe

REVIEW

Exercise 1
is - each
uses - student
do - Joe, Cathy
are - there
is going - Sam, Nancy
is - care, milking
makes - peaches and crème is a unit
is going - everyone
was - end, beginning
has - each

Exercise 2
tastes - lemonade, ice tea
is - chicken and dumplings is a unit
were - Galileo, Copernicus
were - opera hall, baseball stadium
require - mathematics and science

ENGLISH FOUNDATIONS

FOUNDATION VII

VERB TENSE

VERB TENSE tells when something is going on, whether in the past, in the present, or in the future.

The **PRESENT TENSE** usually tells that something is going on right now, or goes on all the time, over and over, or as a habit.

      Example: I <u>am writing</u> a letter home.

      Example: Jack <u>rides</u> his bike to school every day.

The present tense may also tell something that will happen in the future.

      Example: The plane <u>lands</u> in two hours.

EXERCISE 1. <u>Underline</u> the <u>present tense verb</u> or <u>verbs</u> in the following sentences. (Possible Score: 13)

1.   What activities are you doing tomorrow?

2.   Some bacteria are very helpful because they aid in digestion.

3.   If you repeat that remark, I will be angry with you.

4.   When you retire, we will give you a large bonus.

5.   I enjoy reading because it helps me wind down.

6.   I do not have a good memory.

7.   Senators and Representatives make up the Congress of the United States.

8.   He runs a consistent four-minute mile.

9.   The ship sails tomorrow at 7 a.m.

10.   Who knows what the future holds for mankind.

Answers are on page 84. Subtract one point for each incorrect answer. *Your Score:* ____

Exercise 2. <u>Underline</u> the <u>present tense verb</u> or <u>verbs</u> in the following sentences. (Possible Score: 7)

1.   Each of the problems on this test takes about ten minutes to solve.

2.   Neither of your arguments is very convincing.

3.   No one who drives is exempt from the laws of the road.

4.   Only one of the contestants can win the contest.

5.   Airplanes that have radar can fly in any kind of weather.

Answers are on page 84. Subtract one point for each incorrect answer. *Your Score:* _____

APPLICATION. Write 5 sentences using present tense verbs. Underline the past tense verb or verbs in each sentence

1._____

2._____

3._____

4._____

5._____

The **PAST TENSE** says that something happened in the past but is no longer going on. It is finished.

    Example: I <u>spent</u> all my money yesterday.

    Example: Two people <u>drowned</u> when they were swept away by the flood waters.

EXERCISE 1. <u>Underline</u> the <u>past tense verb</u> or <u>verbs</u> in the following sentences.
(Possible Score: 11)

1.   Did you enjoy complete comfort during your stay at our motel?

2.   Mother said not to get your new pants all dirty.

3.   The first settlements by the pioneers were in the wilderness, but they later developed into large cities.

4.   The city announced plans to build a new civic center.

5.   In 1887, George W. Hancock developed softball.

6.	There was nothing to be gained by covering up the theft.

7.	Did you exchange the extra box?

8.	Last Monday was Sharon's birthday.

9.	Bill and John did their work together.

10.	The soda was not frozen.

Answers are on page 84. Subtract one point for each incorrect answer. *Your Score:* ____

EXERCISE 2. Underline the past tense verb or verb in the following sentences. (Possible Score: 6)

1.	The tactical unit attacked swiftly and with force.

2.	The guest speaker arrived just in time for the dinner.

3.	When did the accident happen?

4.	The lifeguard reached the drowning boy just in time.

5.	Did you take out the trash like I asked?

Answers are on page 84. Subtract one point for each incorrect answer. *Your Score:* ____

APPLICATION. Write 5 sentences using past tense verbs. Underline the past tense verb or verbs in each sentence.

1._____

2._____

3._____

4._____

5._____

The **FUTURE TENSE** says that something will happen in the future. These verbs usually include **SHOULD, WOULD, SHALL,** or **WILL**.

Example: We <u>will be leaving</u> on the morning train.

Example: Our flight <u>should be arriving</u> at any moment.

EXERCISE 1. <u>Underline</u> the <u>future tense verb</u> or <u>verbs</u> in the following sentences. (Possible Score: 13)

1.   When will you help me clean this house?

2.   Will you please call me when it is convenient for you?

3.   Shall I call you early tomorrow so you can get an early start?

4.   When should I find out whether I will have the job or not?

5.   Who will take a stand against the forces of evil?

6.   Shall I sing for you, or would you rather I danced?

7.   Jack should not go unless he is called.

8.   Will you stay home this evening for a change?

9.   If I should call, who would answer me?

10.   Jane said that she would pick me up after work.

Answers are on page 85. Subtract one point for each incorrect answer. *Your Score:* _____

EXERCISE 2. <u>Underline</u> the <u>future tense verb</u> or <u>verbs</u> in the following sentences. (Possible Score: 7)

1.   What shall I do with this mess you created?

2.   What would you say if I should decide not to come tonight?

3.   Should you decide to cancel, please call me right away.

4.   Will you return the merchandise you decided not to keep?

5.   I shall tell you what my decision is as soon as I shall make it.

Answers are on page 85. Subtract one point for each incorrect answer. *Your Score:* ____

APPLICATION. Write 5 sentences using future tense verbs. Underline the future tense verb or verbs in each sentence.

1._____

2._____

3._____

4._____

5._____

The **PRESENT PERFECT TENSE** says that something went on in the past but is finished at the present time, or that something went on in the past but is continuing in the present. A clue to the present perfect tense is the use of the helping verb **HAVE** or **HAS** with the main verb.

   Example: I have finished the work I began.

   Example: I have often used the information I learned in college.

EXERCISE 1. Underline the present perfect verb or verbs in the following sentences. (Possible Score: 12)

1.   I have felt for some time that Bob has been wrong.

2.   Have you finished the report I asked you to write?

3.   Have you ever been to Miami Beach in the summertime when it wasn't sweltering?

4.   When have you ever said that you were going to do something great, and you have not done it?

5.   We haven't seen Jane since she left for New York.

6.   Has anyone found my pen that I lost?

7.   I have sung in the Glee Club for five years now.

8.   Cities have changed tremendously since I was a child.

9.   Jack has never been late before.

10.   You must have seen that accident since you were nearby.

Answers are on page 85. Subtract one point for each incorrect answer. *Your Score:* ____

EXERCISE 2. Underline the present perfect verb or verbs in the following sentences. (Possible Score: 6)

1.   How many people have drowned at this overcrowded seashore?

2.   Many people have asked me questions that I simply couldn't have answered.

3.   This shampoo has lasted for a long time.

4.   Have you done the chores you were supposed to do?

5.   What have you done that you later regretted?

Answers are on page 85. Subtract one point for each incorrect answer. *Your Score:* ____

APPLICATION. Write 5 sentences using present perfect verbs. Underline the verb or verbs in each sentence.

1._____

2._____

3._____

4._____

5._____

The **PAST PERFECT TENSE** says that something went on in the past and was finished before a certain time in the past. A clue to the past perfect tense is the use of the helping verb **HAD** with the main verb.

     Example: I had already left when you called.

Example: <u>Had</u> you not <u>written</u>, I would not have known that you were sick.

EXERCISE 1. <u>Underline</u> the <u>past perfect verb</u> or <u>verbs</u> in the following sentences. (Possible Score: 10)

1.   The thieves had already gotten away when the police arrived.

2.   Had you given any thought to my proposal before I just now called?

3.   When had you decided to move to Daytona Beach?

4.   Before I awoke this morning, I had had the strangest dream.

5.   By the time the party started, John had already had too much to drink.

6.   Had you already determined what you would do before I tried to change your mind?

7.   What had you thought about the idea before we discussed it this morning?

8.   She had already fired the gun before we could stop her.

9.   We all know how he had felt about the situation.

10.   Had you not come, I would have been disappointed.

Answers are on page 85. Subtract one point for each incorrect answer. *Your Score:* _____

EXERCISE 2. <u>Underline</u> the <u>past perfect verb</u> or <u>verbs</u> in the following sentences. (Possible Score: 6)

1.   The Indians had attacked the fort before the Cavalry arrived.

2.   Had the earthquake struck during rush hour, there would have been more casualties.

3.   The man had risked his life to save his son by jumping into the river.

4.   Had you asked me that question yesterday, I wouldn't have been able to answer it.

5.   I had already written and sent an e-mail before you called.

Answers are on page 85. Subtract one point for each incorrect answer. *Your Score:* _____

APPLICATION. Write 5 sentences using past perfect verbs. Underline the verb or verbs in each sentence.

1._____

2._____

3._____

4._____

5._____

The **FUTURE PERFECT TENSE** says that something will be finished before a certain time in the future.

    Example: Our letter <u>will have arrived</u> before we get there.

    Example: <u>Will</u> she <u>have finished</u> the letter before she goes home?

EXERCISE 1. <u>Underline</u> the <u>future perfect verb</u> or <u>verbs</u> in the following sentences. (Possible Score: 14)

1.   Your breakfast will have been eaten and you will have had time to read the paper before the sun comes up.

2.   You would have been home in time for me to make my 10 o'clock appointment if the car hadn't broken down.

3.   Would you have come before I called you?

4.   I would have decided that something was wrong if you hadn't come at the usual time.

5.   Before you get here with the cooler of water, we will have practically died of thirst.

6.   I shall have begun to cook supper by the time you will have gotten home.

7.   Would you have thought yesterday that all this would have happened today?

-81-

8. Who would have guessed that she was so pretty?

9. "I shall have come to the end of my life before I will have gotten rich," said the pessimist.

10. Sam will have finished his exam by this time tomorrow.

Answers are on page 86. Subtract one point for each incorrect answer. *Your Score:* _____

EXERCISE 2. Underline the future perfect verb or verbs in the following sentences. (Possible Score: 5)

1. He will have given up all hope of survival if help doesn't arrive soon.

2. Will you have waited for me much longer if I hadn't come when I did?

3. I will have accomplished as much as I can by the time I die.

4. She would have had her novel finished by next Wednesday if she hadn't gotten sick.

5. You will have done all your chores by lunch if you work at it.

Answers are on page 86. Subtract one point for each incorrect answer. *Your Score:* _____

APPLICATION. Write 5 sentences using future perfect verbs. Underline the verb or verbs in each sentence.

1._____

2._____

3._____

4._____

5._____

REVIEW OF FOUNDATION VII

EXERCISE 1. Underline the verbs in the sentences below. Above each verb, write whether it is **PRESENT, PAST, FUTURE, PRESENT PERFECT, PAST PERFECT, OR FUTURE PERFECT TENSE.** (Possible Score: 42)

1. The summer will have been over before you decided to find a job.

2. If you quit your job, you will not be able to collect unemployment benefits.

3. He had suffered for a long time before he finally decided to go into the hospital.

4. I have decided to go to college when I finish high school.

5. Before our life ends, we will have endured many trials and tribulations.

6. I rejoiced to find out that you will be coming to visit us.

7. You will be in trouble if you don't have a good excuse.

8. I had received as many complaints as I could stand when I finally determined that I would take some action.

9. Will you have finished that quilt by the time winter comes?

10. We will pay all these expenses except for food.

Answers are on page 86. Subtract one point for each incorrect answer. *Your Score:* _____

EXERCISE 2. For each sentence, in the blank provided, write the required tense of the verb given in parentheses. (Possible Score: 10)

1. Our team _____ well this year.
    (play - present perfect)

2. I _____ you that I would be on time
    (promise - past)

3. We _____ for Student Council reform.
    (campaign - future)

4. Lisa _____ to buy a car last week.

5.	We _____ ourselves hoarse by the end of the game.
	(cheer - future perfect)

6.	They _____ by the time the storm began.

7.	Peggy _____ the flag in the parade.
	(carry - future)

8.	I _____ working out in the gym.
	(enjoy - present)

9.	Tim _____ in England by evening.
	(land - future perfect)

10.	Renee _____ onto the field before her teammates even
	arrived. (start – past perfect)

Answers on page 86. Subtract one point for each incorrect answer. *Your Score:* _____

ANSWERS TO FOUNDATION VII

PRESENT TENSE

Exercise 1	**Exercise 2**
are doing	takes
are	is
aid	drives
repeat	is
retire	can win
enjoy	have
helps	can
do have	
make up	
runs	
sails	
knows	
holds	

PAST TENSE

Exercise 1	**Exercise 2**
did enjoy	attacked

said
were
developed
announced
developed
was
did exchange
was
did
was

arrived
did happen
reached
did take
asked

FUTURE TENSE

Exercise 1
will help
will call
shall call
should find out
will have
will take
will take
shall sing
would rather
should go
will stay home
should call
would answer
would pick up

Exercise 2
shall do
would say
should decide
should decide
will return
shall tell
shall make

PRESENT PERFECT TENSE

Exercise 1
have felt
has been
have finished
have been
have said
have done
haven't seen
has found
have sung
have changed
has been
must have seen

Exercise 2
have drowned
have asked
couldn't have answered
has lasted
have done
have done

PAST PERFECT TENSE

Exercise 1
had gotten away
had given
had decided
had had
had had
had determined
had thought
had fired
had felt
had come

Exercise 2
had attacked
had struck
had risked
had asked
had written
(had) sent

FUTURE PERFECT TENSE

Exercise 1
will have been eaten
will have had
would have been
would have come
would have decided
will have died
shall have begun
will have gotten
would have thought
would have happened
would have guessed
shall have come
will have gotten
will have finished

Exercise 2
will have given up
will have waited
will have accomplished
would have had
will have done

REVIEW

Exercise 1
will have been - future perfect
decided - past
quit - present
will be able - future
had suffered - past perfect
decided - past
have decided - present perfect
finish - present

Exercise 2
has played
promised
will campaign
decided
will have cheered
had arrived
will carry
enjoy

ends - present
will have endured - future perfect
rejoiced - past
will be coming - future
will be - future
don't have - present
had received - past perfect
could stand - past
determined - past
would take - future
will have finished - future perfect
comes - present
will pay - future

will have landed
had started

FOUNDATION VIII

SUBJECTIVE MOOD

The **SUBJUNCTIVE MOOD** shows doubt, a need, a wish, or something we would like to be true but isn't.

When expressing a wish, or something we would like to be true but isn't, use the subjunctive **WERE**, not **WAS**.

> Example: I wish that Christmas <u>were</u> here already.

> Example: Would that all men <u>were</u> free.

After the phrase **AS IF** and **AS THOUGH**, use the subjunctive **WERE**. Otherwise, use the subjunctive **BE**.

> Example: She acted as if she <u>were</u> the Queen of Sheba.

> Example: <u>Be</u> it ever so humble, there's no place like home.

EXERCISE 1. <u>Underline</u> the <u>subjunctive verb</u> or <u>verbs</u> in the following sentences. (Possible Score: 10)

1. Were I able, I would give you everything I own.

2. He acted as though he were going to pull a gun.

3. I wish I were a bird so I could soar high in the sky.

4. If I were you, I would take the job.

5. Be I rich or poor, I will be content with my God.

6. I wish you were our teacher.

7. I doubt that they were serious about helping us.

8. If you were President of the United States, what would be your goals?

9. Were you to go abroad, you would discover many different cultures.

10. It is necessary that you be available this afternoon.

Answers are on page 91. Subtract one point for each incorrect answer. *Your Score:* ____

EXERCISE 2. <u>Underline</u> the <u>subjunctive verb</u> or <u>verbs</u> in the following sentences. (Possible Score: 5)

1.   I wish I were a doctor so I could heal the sick.

2.   If I were you, I would study hard for the upcoming exam.

3.   I wish he were the President..

4.   He speaks as though he were an authority on the matter.

5.   It was necessary that the criminal be punished to set an example.

Answers are on page 91. Subtract one point for each incorrect answer. *Your Score:* ____

APPLICATION. Write 5 sentences using the subjunctive mood.

1._____

2._____

3._____

4._____

5._____

REVIEW OF FOUNDATION VIII

EXERCISE. <u>Underline</u> the proper word in <u>parentheses</u>. (Possible Score: 10)

1.   I wish that tomorrow (was, were) my birthday.

2.   (Was, were) I free, I would come and help you.

3.   If I (was, were) sure that you weren't deceiving me, I would accept your offer.

4.   It is necessary that she (be, is) punished for what she did.

5.   If I (was, were) mayor, I would make some changes.

Answers are on page 91. Subtract one point for each incorrect answer. *Your Score:* ____

SUBJUNCTIVE MOOD

Exercise 1
were
were
were
were
be
were
were
were
were
be

Exercise 2
were
were
were
be
were

REVIEW

Exercise
were
were
were
be
were

FOUNDATION IX

VERBALS

Words that are usually verbs can sometimes be used the same way as nouns, adjectives, and adverbs. When they are used this way, they are called **VERBALS**. There are three kinds: **PARTICIPLES, GERUNDS,** and **INFINITIVES.**

When a verb ends in **ING, ED,** or some other form of the past tense and is used as an **ADJECTIVE** (to tell something about a noun or pronoun), it is called a **PARTICIPLE.**

Example: The boy <u>standing</u> over there is my brother.

Example: The <u>excited</u> bride dropped her bouquet.

Example: The stars are <u>shining</u> brightly in the clear sky tonight.

EXERCISE 1. <u>Underline</u> the <u>participle</u> or <u>participles</u> in the following sentences. (Possible Score: 40) Put the noun or pronoun to which it refers above it.

1.   A good deed done in love will earn you the respect of everyone.

2.   The flowers growing in the greenhouse are blooming faster than those grown in the garden.

3.   The movie showing downtown has been shown several times before.

4.   Michael is a growing boy who likes to eat everything in sight.

5.   That woman waving her arms is saying something, but I can't hear her.

6.   Standing over here, I can watch the baseball game very well.

7.   Blown by the driving wind, the waves crashed against the seawall with a mighty roar.

8.   The idea, having been suggested by Sam, was voted on and approved by the committee.

9.   I stood there thinking and daydreaming about what could be, if we were willing.

10.   Having accomplished all we had planned, we sailed for home.

Answers are on page 99. Subtract one point for each incorrect answer. *Your Score:* _____

EXERCISE 2. <u>Underline</u> the <u>participle</u> or <u>participles</u> in the following sentences. (Possible Score: 22) Put the noun or pronoun to which it refers above it.

1.   The stream running through the mountains is beautiful.

2.   The broken limb on your car is a result of the severe storm.

3.   The game was exciting.

4.   She was discouraged because she didn't get good grades.

5.   The brook, running swiftly, disappeared around the bend.

6.   My arm, broken by a fall, is healing slowly.

7.   The novel, written in only three weeks, is on the bestseller list.

8.   Running to the window, I saw the fire trucks followed by an ambulance.

9.   By working hard, we accomplish most of what we want.

10.   We enjoyed marshmallows, sitting around the campfire.

Answers are on page 99. Subtract one point for each incorrect answer. *Your Score:* ____

APPLICATION. Write 5 sentences using participles. Underline the participles in your sentences.

1._____

2._____

3._____

4._____

5._____

When a verb ends in **ING** and is used as a **NOUN** (as the subject or object of a verb, or as the object of a preposition) it is called a **GERUND**. It sometimes requires careful observation to distinguish the gerund from a participle, especially when they both end in -**ING**.

Example: <u>Swimming</u> is a lot of fun in the summertime. (<u>Swimming</u> is the subject of the verb <u>is</u>.)

Example: There are other ways of <u>doing</u> things. (<u>Doing</u> is the object of the preposition of.)

EXERCISE 1. <u>Underline</u> the <u>gerund</u> or <u>gerunds</u> in the following sentences. (Possible Score: 13)

1.   Daydreaming will not get you what you want or need.

2.   Some people, desiring to get in shape, think that jogging is the best way to do so.

3.   Running for public office takes much more money and effort than effort than it used to.

4.   I have decided that throwing a party is not the only way of having fun.

5.   I find that flying provides an enjoyable means of relaxing.

6.   My favorite hobby is sky diving.

7.   I heard the whispering of the wind in the treetops while I was camping in the forest.

8.   Do you enjoy mountain climbing?

9.   Painting the house is not my idea of recreating.

10.   I am taking a course in creative writing because I am working on my degree in English.

Answers are on page 100. Subtract one point for each incorrect answer. *Your Score:* ___

EXERCISE 2. <u>Underline</u> the <u>gerund</u> or <u>gerunds</u> in the following sentences. (Possible Score: 6)

1.   Taking what doesn't belong to you is wrong.

2.   Sleeping in class will keep you from learning what you need to.

3.   Do you object to smoking as long as I do it outside?

4.   Painting houses is my artistic skill.

5.   My wife's artistic skill is painting pictures.

Answers are on page 100. Subtract one point for each incorrect answer. *Your Score:* ___

APPLICATION. Write 5 sentences using gerunds. Underline the gerunds in your sentences.

1._____

2._____

3._____

4._____

5._____

When a verb is preceded by the word **TO**, it is an **INFINITIVE**.

    Example: We like to play baseball.

    Example: I would like to have gone with you.

An infinitive can be used as a **NOUN** and so can be used as the subject of a verb, for example, just like any other noun. Remember that nouns answer the question **WHAT?**.

    Example: To succeed in business is very difficult. (To succeed is the subject of the verb is.)

    Example: He desired to go with his dad to the beach. (To go is the object of the verb desired.)

An infinitive can be used as an **ADJECTIVE**, telling something about a noun or pronoun.

    Example: I have twenty-five cows to be sold at auction. (To be sold describes the cows.)

    Example: To be successful, a person needs a lot of drive. (To be successful describes a person.)

An infinitive can be used as an **ADVERB**, answering the question **WHY, WHEN, HOW, WHERE,** or **HOW MUCH.**

Example: Many rushed <u>to see</u> what was going on. (<u>To see</u> tells <u>why</u> many rushed.)

Example: My aunt came <u>to visit</u> us last week.)

EXERCISE 1. <u>Underline</u> the <u>infinitive</u> or <u>infinitives</u> in the following sentences. <u>Above each</u> one, put **N** if the infinitive is used as a <u>noun</u>, **ADJ** if used as an <u>adjective</u>, and **ADV** if used as an <u>adverb</u>. (Possible Score: 24)

1.   I am planning to go to the doctor this Friday.

2.   There is a job to be done, and everyone needs to pitch in.

3.   You just said that to make me feel better.

4.   My greatest desire is to see you happy.

5.   We have little time to spare before the bus comes.

6.   I ought to have been here when you came, but I had to run an emergency errand.

7.   He obtained a loan to go into business.

8.   Can you find a way to get to school tomorrow?

9.   Shelly hoped to have finished the painting before you came.

10.   I have longed to meet you for some time now.

Answers are on page 100. Subtract one point for each incorrect answer. *Your Score:* ___

EXERCISE 2. <u>Underline</u> the <u>infinitive</u> or <u>infinitives</u> in the following sentences. <u>Above each</u> one, put **N** if it is used as a noun, **ADJ** if it is used as an adjective, or **ADV** if it is used as an adverb. (Possible Score: 10)

1.   He wishes to call you for a date.

2.   What we really want is to win the trophy.

3.   Mary likes to write short stories.

4.   You are not allowed to go there.

5.   Be ready to go at 8 o'clock.

Answers are on page 100. Subtract one point for each incorrect answer. *Your Score:* ___

APPLICATION. Write 5 sentences using infinitives. Above each, put **N, ADJ**, or **ADV** as in the above exercises.

1._____

2._____

3._____

4._____

5._____

REVIEW OF FOUNDATION IX

EXERCISE 1. Underline the verbals in the following sentences. Above each one put **P** if it is a participle, **G** if it is a gerund, and **I** if it is an infinitive. (Possible Score: 46)

1.   Desiring to swim will not teach you how; you have to jump into the water.

2.   The water boiling on the hot stove is to put moisture into the air to reduce the dryness.

3.   Winding lazily through the field, the babbling brook finally empties into a mighty river.

4.   To live in peace is the goal of every civilized nation.

5.   Fishing and swimming are two relaxing ways to enjoy a summer afternoon.

6.   Standing at the lookout, you can see for miles across the mountains.

7.   Charging into the ring, the bull attempted immediately to gorge the matador.

8.   Changing diapers and bottle feeding are two frequent chores of parenthood.

9.   Wishing to have been there earlier, Madge arrived twenty minutes late for her appointment.

10. Hindered at first by a lack of funds and materials, Joe seems now to have succeeded in building his boat.

Answers are on page 101. Subtract one point for each incorrect answer. *Your Score:* ___

EXERCISE 2. Underline the verbals in the following sentences. Above each one put **P** if it is a participle, **G** if it is a gerund, and **I** if it is an infinitive. (Possible Score: 30)

1. Everyone enjoys Arturo's wry humor and smiling face.

2. Mountaineering and sky diving are sports for hearty souls.

3. Charlie made a diving catch to end an exciting game.

4. To some people, a foreign language is difficult to learn.

5. Clint took the frozen dinners out of the freezer.

6. I have so much homework to do before we go to the movie.

7. The photography instructor said that we would probably need her help with the first step, developing, and the last step, enlarging.

8. We could hear the sound of laughing in the distance.

9. I plan to graduate in three years.

10 We set the table with the cleaned and polished silver and the sparkling glasses.

Answers are on page 101. Subtract one point for each incorrect answer. *Your Score:* ___

ANSWERS TO FOUNDATION IX

PARTICIPLES

Exercise 1
done -deed
growing - flowers
blooming - flowers
grown - flowers (understood)
showing - movie
shown - movie

Exercise 2
running -stream
broken - limb
exciting - game
discouraged - she
running - brook
broken - arm

growing - boy
waving - woman
saying - woman
standing - I
blown - waves
driving - wind
having been suggested - idea
voted on - idea
approved - idea
thinking - I
daydreaming - I
willing - we
accomplished - we
planned - we

written - novel
running - I
followed - trucks
working - we
sitting - we

GERUNDS

Exercise 1
daydreaming
jogging
running
throwing
having
flying
relaxing
sky diving
whispering
mountain climbing
painting
recreating
creative writing

Exercise 2
taking
sleeping
learning
smoking
painting
painting

INFINITIVES

Exercise 1
to go - N
to be done - ADJ
to pitch in - N
to make - ADV
to see - N
to spare - ADJ
to have been - N
to run - N

Exercise 2
to call - N
to win - N
to write - N
to go - N
to go - ADV

to go - ADJ
to get - ADJ
to have finished - N
to meet - N

REVIEW

Exercise 1
desiring - G
to swim - I
to jump - I
boiling - P
to put - I
to reduce - I
winding - P
babbling - P
to live - I
fishing - G
swimming - G
relaxing - P
to enjoy - I
standing - P
charging - P
to gorge - I
changing - G
bottle feeding - G
wishing - P
to have been - I
hindered - P
to have succeeded - I
building - G

Exercise 2
smiling -P
mountaineering - G
sky diving - G
diving - P
exciting - P
to learn - I
frozen - P
to do - I
developing - G
enlarging - G
laughing - G
to graduate - I
cleaned - P
polished - P
sparkling - P

ENGLISH FOUNDATIONS

FOUNDATION X

OBJECTS

The **DIRECT OBJECT** always answers **WHAT** or **WHOM** after an action verb. It can be a noun, pronoun, gerund, or infinitive.

Example: I bought a new <u>car</u> last week.

Example: I have decided <u>to follow</u> God's ways.

Example: Will you milk the <u>cow</u> this morning.

Example: I really enjoy <u>sailing</u>.

EXERCISE 1. <u>Underline</u> the <u>direct object</u> or <u>objects</u> in the following sentences. (Possible Score: 13)

1. At the farmers' market, we bought eggs, lettuce, cabbage, and onions.

2. Your mother said to clean your room.

3. I enjoy hunting in the fall.

4. Sarah made herself a wool blanket.

5. Would you take him to work tomorrow?

6. I said I would give a donation to charity.

7. Are you planning anything for the Fourth of July?

8. The furnace was not heating the house very well.

9. I keep losing my key.

10. Do you like listening to classical music?

Answers are on page 107. Subtract one point for each incorrect answer. *Your Score:* ___

EXERCISE 2. <u>Underline</u> the <u>direct object</u> or <u>objects</u> in the following sentences. (Possible Score:)

1. Farmers in North Carolina grow tobacco as a major crop.

2. We went to a performance of *Man of La Mancha*.

3.   The whole neighborhood held a cookout last night.

4.   Would you please answer the telephone.

5.   Be sure to turn off the computer when you are finished.

6.   Who invited her to the party?

7.   Archeologists keep finding older and older human skulls.

8.   Have you and your fiancé set a date for your wedding yet?

9.   I can listen to good music for hours.

10.   Would you please give me your opinion about my writing?

Answers are on page 107. Subtract one point for each incorrect answer. *Your Score:* ___

APPLICATION. Write 5 sentences using direct objects. Underline the direct object in each sentence.

1._____

2._____

3._____

4._____

5._____

An **INDIRECT OBJECT** answers **TO WHOM, TO WHAT, FOR WHOM,** or **FOR WHAT** the verb was done. Sometimes it has <u>to</u> or <u>for</u> before it, but often these are simply understood.. Sentences may have both direct objects and indirect objects in them. Normally, the indirect object goes before the direct object, but not always.

EXERCISE 1. <u>Underline</u> the <u>indirect object</u> or <u>objects</u> in the following sentences. (Possible Score: 11)

1.   Give me a break!

2.   Give that book back to her right now before I punish you.

3. I would like to buy you a new coat.

4. Would you please give me directions to your house?

5. I would like to give you a piece of my mind.

6. Would you please bring a sandwich to me when you come back from lunch?

7. This job will be good for you and for me.

8. It is good for us to be here, Lord.

9. If you know what is good for you, you will come home right away.

10. He gave a diamond ring to his girlfriend last night.

Answers are on page 107. Subtract one point for each incorrect answer. *Your Score:* ___

EXERCISE 2. Underline the indirect object or objects in the following sentences. (Possible Score: 6)

1. The teacher told us what was expected for the next test.

2. I want to do something special for you for your birthday.

3. Do only to others what you would have them do to you.

4. We gave her a gold watch for her graduation.

5. The son sent his mother some of his earnings each paycheck.

Answers are on page 107. Subtract one point for each incorrect answer. *Your Score:* ___

APPLICATION. Write 5 sentences using indirect objects. Underline the indirect objects in each sentence.

1._____

2._____

3._____

4._____

5._____

REVIEW OF FOUNDATION X

EXERCISE 1. In the following sentences, put **DO** above the direct object or objects and **IO** above the indirect object or objects. (Possible Score: 13)

1.   Please tell us your secret.

2.   I gave a quart of milk to my neighbor.

3.   I don't mind studying when it is quiet.

4.   Bill has not done his work.

5.   The government will prosecute corrupt public servants whenever it can.

6.   Do they regard you as a candidate for election?

7.   You should prepare to return to work as soon as possible.

8.   If you improve your work, I will promote you.

9.   Do pigs have teeth?

10.   That sneaky person over there bears watching.

Answers are on page 108. Subtract one point for each incorrect answer. *Your Score:* ___

EXERCISE 2. In the following sentences, put **DO** above the direct object or objects and **IO** above the indirect object or objects. (Possible Score: 10)

1.   His father wired him the money he requested.

2.   The policeman directed me to the public library.

3.   Would you show me the best restaurants in this area?

4.   Somebody gave you bad advice about your finances.

5.   We took our relatives some oranges when we went home at Christmas.

Answers are on page 108. Subtract one point for each incorrect answer. *Your Score:* ___

ANSWERS TO FOUNDATION X

DIRECT OBJECTS

Exercise 1
eggs
lettuce
cabbage
onions
to clean
hunting
blanket
him
donation
anything
house
key
listening

Exercise 2
tobacco
performance
cookout
telephone
computer
her
skulls
date
music
opinion

INDIRECT OBJECTS

Exercise 1
me
to her
you
me
you
to me
for you
for me
for us
for you
to girlfriend

Exercise 2
us
for you
to others
to you
her
mother

REVIEW

Exercise 1
us - IO
secret - DO
milk - DO
neighbor - IO
studying - DO
work - DO
servants - DO
you - DO
to return - DO
work - DO
you - DO
teeth - DO
watching – DO

Exercise 2
him - IO
money - DO
me - DO
public library - IO
me - IO
restaurants - DO
you - IO
advice - DO
relatives - IO
oranges - DO

ENGLISH FOUNDATIONS

FOUNDATION XI

SUBJECT COMPLEMENTS

The **SUBJECT COMPLEMENT** finishes the meaning of the verb. It explains or tells something about the subject. Subject complements may be nouns, pronouns, or adjectives.

> Example: Those flowers are <u>beautiful</u>. (Adjective)

> Example: John is <u>President</u> of the student council. (Noun)

> Example: It was <u>you</u> who hid my book. (Pronoun)

Subject complements are most often linked by some form of the verb *be* such as *am, is, was, were.* However, some other verbs can also be used such as *seem, become, appear, prove, look, remain, feel, taste, smell sound, turn, grow.*

> Example: This task proved more difficult than we first thought.

> Example: The peaches turned rotten much faster than they should have.

EXERCISE 1. <u>Underline</u> the <u>subject complement</u> or in the following sentences. (Possible Score: 10)

1.   My mother's soup tastes delicious.

2.   In God's care we become safe.

3.   Football is a rough sport

4.   Everyone seemed to be happy about our chance of winning.

5.   That sounds like a very poor excuse.

6.   This child looks very mischievous.

7.   I feel awful.

8.   Who is that man looking in the window?

9.   Jane is a new student in our class.

10.   Dogs are very playful.

Answers are on page 112. Subtract one point for each incorrect answer. *Your Score:* __

EXERCISE 2. Underline the subject complement in the following sentences. (Possible Score: 5)

1.   Many people become angry at life as they get older.

2.   Things often appear quite different upon closer inspection.

3.   You look much better now than you did earlier.

4.   It remains unclear whether she did it or didn't

5.   Music sounds much clearer when it is not played so loudly.

Answers are on page 112. Subtract one point for each incorrect answer. *Your Score:* ___

APPLICATION. Write 10 sentences using a variety of linking verbs. Underline the subject complement in each sentence.

1._____

2._____

3._____

4._____

5._____

6._____

7._____

8._____

9._____

10._____

REVIEW OF FOUNDATION XI

EXERCISE. Underline the subject complements in the following sentences. Above each one, put **N** if it is a noun, **P** if it is a pronoun, or **A** if it is an adjective. (Possible Score: 24)

1. A man's home is his castle.

2. The early pioneers became very courageous and resourceful as they moved across the country.

3. Golf seems to be good exercise after a day's work.

4. Who is she to tell me off like that?

5. Overeating would seem to be harmful to good health for most people.

6. The hawk is a mighty bird of prey.

7. In the sight of God, we are proved to be equal.

8. Orville and Wilber Wright became the first inventors of the airplane to actually fly.

9. Many are called but few are chosen.

10. Washington, D.C. became the capital of the United States.

Answers are on page 113. Subtract one point for each incorrect answer. *Your Score:* ___

ANSWERS TO FOUNDATION XI

SUBJECT COMPLEMENTS

Exercise 1	**Exercise 2**
delicious	angry
safe	different
sport	better
happy	unclear
excuse	clearer
mischievous	
awful	
man	
student	
playful	

REVIEW

Exercise.
castle - N
courageous - A
resourceful - A
exercise - N
she - P
harmful - A
bird - N
equal - A
inventors - N
called - A
chosen - A
capital - N

ENGLISH FOUNDATIONS

FOUNDATION XII

ADVERBS

An **ADVERB** is a word that tells something about a verb, an adjective, or another adverb. Adverbs usually answer the question **WHEN, WHERE, HOW, HOW MUCH** or **HOW OFTEN**. Adverbs often end in **-LY**, but not always.

Example: The box is <u>extremely</u> heavy. (<u>Extremely</u> tells <u>how</u> heavy the box is)

Example: The stream flows <u>rapidly</u> at this point. (<u>Rapidly</u> tells <u>how much</u> the stream flows)

EXERCISE 1. <u>Underline</u> the <u>adverb</u> or <u>adverbs</u> in the following sentences. (Possible Score: 12)

1.   Ralph laughed out loud.

2.   You pleased me very much.

3.   Yesterday I discovered the mine.

4.   Now is the time for all good men to defend their country.

5.   The doctor detected a rapidly beating heart.

6.   Henry called you earlier in the day.

7.   Slowly I raised the lid on the mysterious box.

8.   Pile those bricks over here.

9.   Ann scattered the seeds everywhere.

10.   As quickly as possible, he explained the plan and then hurriedly left.

Answers are on page 117. Subtract one point for each incorrect answer. *Your Score:* ___

EXERCISE 2. <u>Underline</u> the <u>adverb</u> or <u>adverbs</u> in the following sentences. (Possible Score: 15)

1.   She walked up proudly to receive her diploma.

2.   John left yesterday for his trip to Alaska.

3.   Some of my friends went there and others stayed here.

4. He walked very slowly off the field after he was hit.

5. The birds came only once and we never saw them again.

6. Whoever arrives first at the finish line is the winner.

7. She smiled joyfully after receiving the award.

8. She performed beautifully at her first recital.

9. The little girl ran playfully alongside her mother.

10. We were almost there when our tire went flat.

Answers are on page 117. Subtract one point for each incorrect answer. *Your Score:* ___

APPLICATION. Write 5 sentences using adverbs. Underline the adverb in each sentence.

1._____

2._____

3._____

4._____

5._____

REVIEW OF FOUNDATION XII

EXERCISE. Underline the adverb or adverbs in the following sentences. Above each one write whether they answer the question **WHEN, HOW, WHERE, HOW MUCH** or **HOW OFTEN**. (Possible Score: 28)

1. Dorothy lingered nearby.

2. Today our two kittens were killed.

3. You are unnecessarily concerned about my health.

4. You seldom hear any good reports on the news anymore.

5. The troops fought fiercely and determinedly.

6. We need help now.

7. The dogs howled loudly all night.

8. The medics worked frantically over the victim as the police patrolled nearby.

9. You often hear stories that are exaggerated and untrue.

10. The thunder rumbled loudly over the plain as the storm clouds rapidly developed.

Answers are on page 117. Subtract one point for each incorrect answer. *Your Score:* ___

ANSWERS TO FOUNDATION XII

ADVERBS

Exercise 1
out loud
very
much
yesterday
now
rapidly
earlier
slowly
here
everywhere
quickly
hurriedly

Exercise 2
proudly
yesterday
there
here
slowly
only
once
never
again
first
joyfully
beautifully
playfully
alongside
there

REVIEW

Exercise
nearby - where
today - when

Exercise (cont.)
frantically - how
nearby - where

unnecessarily - how much
seldom - how often
loudly – how
anymore - when
fiercely - how
determinedly - how
now - when
loudly - how

often - when

rapidly - how

ENGLISH FOUNDATIONS

FOUNDATION XIII

PREPOSITIONS

A **PREPOSITION** is a word, or group of words, put before a noun or pronoun to explain, describe, or complete the meaning of some other word in the sentence.

Example: Go <u>through</u> the door <u>into</u> the kitchen and you will find her.

Example: <u>In spite of</u> our best efforts, we lost the game.

The noun or pronoun after the preposition is called the **OBJECT** of the preposition. The object of the preposition may or not be expressed.

Example: He came <u>to a large tree</u> and scrambled <u>up</u>.

Example: When he left the house, he left the porch light on.

Some of the prepositions that are used most often are as follows:

aboard	below	in spite of	through
about	beneath	instead of	throughout
above	beside	into	to
according to	between	near	toward
across	beyond	of	under
after	by	off	underneath
against	down	on	until
along	during	on account of	unto
amid	except	out of	up
among	for	outside	upon
around	from	over	with
at	from among	past	within
because of	from between	round	without
before	from under	round about	
behind	in	since	

EXERCISE 1. <u>Underline</u> the <u>preposition</u> or <u>prepositions</u> in the following sentences. (Possible Score: 24)

1. We have been friends since last September.

2. Be thankful for what you have.

3. All of the exhibits at the museum were stolen during the night.

4. Many people keep their homes cooler in the summertime.

5. We drove through the mountains and over the hills to get to our vacation resort.

6. If you will look underneath the pile of papers in the garage, you will find what you are seeking.

7. It is difficult for me to extract myself from between the sheets in the morning.

8. Out beyond the barn and over the next fencerow you will find sheep grazing amid the hogs.

9. Passengers aboard this flight are among the friendliest I have had within my memory.

10. Throughout our lifetime, we will find ourselves under trials of various kinds.

Answers are on page 124. Subtract one point for each incorrect answer. *Your Score:* ___

EXERCISE 2. <u>Underline</u> the <u>preposition</u> or <u>prepositions</u> in the following sentences. (Possible Score: 15)

1. Because of all the rain we have been having, farmers have been unable to get into their fields.

2. God has brought us out of darkness and into his marvelous light.

3. I would like you to buy this dress instead of that one.

4. The quarterback continued to play in spite of the pain from being hit.

5. Throughout his career, he continued to play brilliantly.

6. We continued to fight against all odds.

7. Many people continue to spend beyond their means, which only gets them deeper into debt.

8.   I will drop you off at the nearest crosswalk.

9.   You will have many difficulties to face during your lifetime.

10.   According to our records, you have not made a payment on your account this
        month.

Answers are on page 124. Subtract one point for each incorrect answer. *Your Score:* ___

APPLICATION. Write 10 sentences using a variety of prepositions. Underline the
prepositions in each sentence.

1._____

2._____

3._____

4._____

5._____

6._____

7._____

8._____

9._____

10._____

REVIEW OF FOUNDATION XIII

EXERCISE 1. In the following sentences, <u>underline</u> each <u>preposition once</u>, and the <u>noun</u>
or <u>pronoun</u> that goes with it <u>twice</u>. (Possible Score: 43)

1.   Over the river and through the woods to Grandmother's house we go.

2.   She said to him, "I would like to go with you to the dance, but around the end of
        the day I am just too tired.

3.   During my stay here in New York, I found myself round and about a large variety of cultural and ethnic groups.

4.   Pick any from among those gifts on the shelf except the ones on the left side between the first and last sections.

5.   Besides them, who else will be going on the cruise around the cape and underneath the African continent?

Answers are on page 124. Subtract one point for each incorrect answer. *Your Score:* ___

EXERCISE 2. Do the same as above. (Possible Score: 18)

THE SPANGLED PANDEMONIUM

-by Mike Parsons

The Spangled Pandemonium

     is missing from the Zoo.

He bent the bars the barest bit

     And slithered glibly through.

He crawled across the moated wall

     And climbed the mango tree.

And, when his keeper scrambled up,

     He nipped him in the knee.

To all of you a warning heed:

     Don't wander after dark

Or, if you must, make sure you stay

     Away from Hanson's Park

The Spangled Pandemonium

     Is missing from the Zoo.

And, since he nipped his keeper,

He would just as soon nip you.

Answers are on page 124. Subtract one point for each incorrect answer. *Your Score:* ___

ANSWERS TO FOUNDATION XIII

PREPOSITIONS

Exercise 1
since
for
of
at
during
in
through
over
to
underneath
of
in
for
from between
in
beyond
over
amid
aboard
among
within
throughout
under
of

Exercise 2
because of
into
out of
into
instead of
in spite of
from
throughout
against
beyond
into
at
during
according to
on

REVIEW

Exercise 1
<u>over</u> <u>river</u>
_____

<u>through</u> <u>woods</u>
_____

<u>to</u> <u>house</u>
_____

Exercise 2
<u>from</u> zoo
___

<u>through</u>
___

<u>across</u> <u>wall</u>
___

to him
___

with you
___

to dance
___

around end
___

of day
___

during stay
___

in New York
___

round about variety
___

of groups
___

from among gifts
___

on shelf
___

except ones
___

on side
___

between sections
___

besides them
___

on cruise
___

around cape
___

underneath continent
___

up

in knee
___

to all
___

of you
___

after dark
___

away from Hanson's Park
___

from Zoo
___

ENGLISH FOUNDATIONS

FOUNDATION XIV

CAPITALIZATION

The first word of every sentence is always **CAPITALIZED**. Capitalize the first word and each **IMPORTANT WORD** in the title of a book, booklet, song, or story.

> Example: Ode to Joy

> Example: A Day in the Life of Miss Jane Spencer

> Example: Fundamentals of Gardening

Capitalize the first word of each line of a poem.

> Example: Ol' Pa, from the country, and Ma
> Went in a Bostonian Spa.
> Did they have a fit
> When they found that it
> Was a sweet-shop instead of a bar.

Capitalize important words in the greeting of a letter and the first word of the complimentary close of a letter.

> Example: Dear Mom and Dad

> Example: To Whom It May Concern

> Example: Sincerely,

> Example: Yours Truly,

Capitalize the first word of a direct quotation.

> Example: Mother said, "There are still Kings who sit on thrones in some countries."

> Example: Michelle exclaimed, "How beautiful the music is!"

Capitalize the names of buildings.

> Example: Your classes will be held in the Arts and Science Building.

> Example: Have you seen the United Nations Building?

Capitalize the names of churches, synagogues, mosques, and religious denominations.

Example: The convention was attended by Baptists, Methodists, and Catholics.

Example: Sam attended Temple Israel.

Capitalize the names of countries, languages, and nationalities.

Example: When we went to Europe, we visited France, Germany, and Switzerland.

Example: Do you speak Spanish fluently?

Example: The Chinese and Russians signed a new peace treaty.

Capitalize the names of the days of the week, the months of the year, and special days.

Example: Let's get together for lunch next Tuesday.

Example: August is the hottest month of the year.

Example: Are you going to the race on Memorial Day?

Capitalize the names of firms and businesses.

Example: There is a sale at Dunn Brothers Lumber Company

Example: We do our banking at Bradford Bank and Trust.

Capitalize the names of persons.

Example: I'd like you to meet Mr. Steve Reynolds.

Example: Joe Stanley is my brother-in-law.

Capitalize the names of mountains, streams, rivers, oceans, lakes, seas, bays, and gulfs.

Example: The tropical storm hit the Gulf of Mexico.

Example: We visited the Blue Ridge Mountains last summer.

Capitalize the names of schools.

Example: Mike attended Spruce Creek High School.

Example: Penny and I are graduates of Ball State University.

Capitalize the names of streets, states, towns, and cities.

Example: He lives on Elm Street in Tincup, Indiana.

Example: We are now residents of North Carolina.

Capitalize the pronoun I

Capitalize the titles of people.

Example: May I introduce our Secretary of State, Mr. Nelson.

Example: Senator Brown is the new Speaker of the House.

Example: We went to visit Aunt Mary and Uncle John.

Capitalize the Bible and its books, the Koran, and names given to the Deity (God, Yahweh, Allah, Lord).

Example: Have you read the Book of Ruth?

Example: The Koran is the holy book of the Moslem people.

Example: We are to praise and worship Almighty God.

Capitalize initials and the abbreviation of a person's name.

Example: T. S. Eliot was a famous poet.

Example: Wm. H. Harrison was President of the United States.

Capitalize abbreviations of a title that is written as part of a name.

Example: The pastor's name is Rev. Robert Jones.

Example: Sen. Richard Stone spoke at the testimonial dinner.

Capitalize the two letters in the state address that precede the zip code.

Example: Millers Creek, NC 28651

EXERCISE 1. In the following sentences, <u>underline each letter</u> that should be <u>capitalized</u> and <u>write above</u> it the <u>capital letter</u>. (Possible Score: 114)

1. sally, don't your grandparents live in san francisco?

2. pete and i are going to the paramount theater on bixford street.

3. the declaration of independence was signed on july 4, 1778.

4. the ohio river forms the boundary between indiana and kentucky.

5. john said, "why can't jerry and i go with uncle henry?'

6. the st. lawrence seaway connects the great lakes with the atlantic ocean.

7. the lot at the corner of cherry avenue and second street was bought by dr. r. j. sanford.

8. mark twain wrote "the adventures of tom sawyer."

9. columbus crossed the atlantic ocean with the nina, the pinta, and the santa maria.

10.   my favorite subjects are math and science.

Answers are on page 132. Subtract one point for each incorrect answer. *Your Score:* ___

EXERCISE 2. Do the same as the above exercise. (Possible Score: 72)

1. poems are made by fools like me,

    but only god can make a tree.

2. the fireman shouted, "hit the floor and head for the door!"

3. we are getting ready for the fourth of july celebrations.

4. sally graduated from millers creek high school and will be attending asu in the fall.

5. my sister-in-law belongs to the d.a.r.

6.   the crossword puzzle in the new york times is very difficult for most people.

7.   the president of the united states is visiting our area this saturday.

8.   many people do not remember the korean war.

9.   he shouted, "hey, wait for me!"

10.   wm. is the abbreviation for william.

Answers are on page 132. Subtract one point for each incorrect answer. *Your Score:* ___

APPLICATION. Write 10 sentences using a variety of capitals. Underline the capitalized words in each sentence.

1._____

2._____

3._____

4._____

5._____

6._____

7._____

8._____

9._____

10._____

REVIEW OF FOUNDATION XIV

EXERCISE 1. Underline each letter that should be capitalized. Write above it the capital letter. (Possible Score: 28)

1.   the capital of argentina is buenos aires.

2.   it is located on the coast of the atlantic ocean.

3.   the western region includes the andes mountains.

4.   the parana river and its tributaries form a large river system.

5.   argentina is big, compared with the countries surrounding it.

Answers are on page 133. Subtract one point for each incorrect answer. *Your Score:* ___

EXERCISE 2. Underline each letter that should be capitalized. Write above it the capital letter. (Possible Score: 48)

924 elmwood avenue

white oak, il 60605

tuesday, june 14, 2003

dear rev. jones:

I was reading the bible, in the gospel of st. john, that god the father so loved the world that he sent his own son to die for it. that means you and me, too. i'm glad god really loves me that much. that is the real gift we receive on christmas day, isn't it?

your friend,

jenny

Answers are on page 133. Subtract one point for each incorrect answer. *Your Score:* ___

ANSWERS TO FOUNDATION XIV

CAPITALIZATION

Exercise 1
Sally
San Francisco
Pete

Exercise 2
Poems
But
God

I
Paramount Theater
Bixrford Street
The
Declaration of Independence
July
The
Ohio River
Indiana
Kentucky
John
Why
Jerry
I
Uncle Henry
The
St. Lawrence Seaway
Great Lakes
Atlantic Ocean
The
Cherry Avenue
Second Street
Dr. R. J. Sanford
Mark Twain
The Adventures of Tom Sawyer
Columbus
Atlantic Ocean
Nina, Pinta, Santa Maria
My
Math
Science

The
Hit
We
Fourth of July
Sally
Millers Creek High School
A S U
My
D. A. R
The
New York Times
The
President.
United States
Saturday
Many
Korean War
He
Hey
Wm.
William

REVIEW

Exercise 1
The
Argentina
Buenos Aires
It
Atlantic Ocean
The
Andes Mountains
The

Exercise 2
Elmwood Avenue
White Oak, IL
Tuesday
June
Dear Rev. Jones
Bible
Gospel
St. John

Parana River
Argentina

God
Father
That
I'm
God
That
Christmas Day
Your
Jenny

ENGLISH FOUNDATIONS

FOUNDATION XV

COMMAS

A **COMMA** goes between the name of a town or city and the name of the state it is in.

Example: My family lives in Lafayette, Indiana

Example: Detroit, Michigan is the automobile capital of the United States.

A comma goes before or after the name of a person to whom you are speaking.

Example: Susie, would you please shut the door?

Example: I'll be with you soon, Pam.

A comma is used to set off other words like **YES** and **NO** when they answer a question **AND** are followed by other words.

Example: Will you help me? Yes, as soon as I finish this last bite.

Example: No, you may not go.

Words like **OH, AH, WELL, WHY,** and **NOW** are followed by a comma when they begin a sentence but aren't really necessary.

Example: Well, you never know what might happen.

Example: Why, I was just there yesterday.

A comma goes between the day of the month and the year.

Example: Today is June 21, 2003.

A comma goes after someone's last name when it is written before the first name.

Example: You will find the book listed under Johnson, Arthur.

A comma goes just before, or just after, a direct quotation.

Example: Carole said, "Help me wash the dishes."

Example: "Is your pen out of ink?" asked Lydia.

A comma goes after the greeting, and just before your name at the close of a friendly letter.

Example: Dear Jane,

Example: Your friend, Sally

A comma goes between the words, or group of words, in a series.

Example: Jim, Jerry, Tom, and I are good friends.

Example: Lock the doors, close the windows, and turn off all the lights before you leave.

EXERCISE 1. Put a comma in the proper place in the following sentences. (Possible Score: 17)

1. Bobby exclaimed "How hot this soup is!"

2. Well if you have to I guess it is alright.

3. Now where did I put my glasses?

4. The letter was sent to Baxter Jerry in Seymore Georgia on September 10 2002

5. I have to go to the grocery pay some bills and get some gas before supper.

6. "Are you going to the picnic?" "No I have to work."

7. What time will you be home Jack.

8. Oh go ahead and eat without me.

9. "Be sure to wear your orange and black jacket tomorrow" said Dick.

10. Argentina Brazil Chile Peru Bolivia and Paraguay are in South America.

Answers are on page 135. Subtract one point for each incorrect answer. *Your Score:* ___

EXERCISE 2. Put a comma in the proper place in the following sentences. (Possible Score: 7)

1. We came we saw we conquered.

2. Ah well I might as well go home.

3.	Charlie will you please help me with this tire?

4.	Sarah came from Seymore Indiana yesterday.

5.	I was born on March 25 1939.

Answers are on page 135. Subtract one point for each incorrect answer. *Your Score:* ____

APPLICATION. Write 5 sentences using commas.

1._____

2._____

3._____

4._____

5._____

PHRASES and **CLAUSES** are additional groups of words that help to make a sentence clearer or more interesting. Commas are often used to separate less important material from more important material.

Less important material is a phrase or clause that could be left out without changing the meaning of the main sentence.

> Example: Leonard da Vinci, who is known for his painting "The Betrayal by Judas", was a fantastic inventor. (Leonardo da Vinci was a fantastic inventor would make sense by itself, so the clause who is known…. is less important and is set off by commas.)

Important material is that which is necessary for the sentence to make sense.

> Example: Students who study will learn more than students who don't. (The phrase who study is important because the sentence wouldn't make sense without it.)

If you are not sure whether a phrase or clause is important or not, try leaving it out. If the sentence still makes sense without it, use commas.

An **APPOSITIVE** is a phrase or clause that goes immediately after a noun or pronoun and further describes it.

Commas are placed before and after an appositive and the word that describes it to set it off from the rest of the sentence.

Example: Mr. Wilson, the friendly banker, lives down the street from us. (The friendly banker further describes Mr. Wilson.)

Example: Miss Kelly, my geography and home room teacher, is the author of three books on travel. (My geography and home room teacher further describes Miss Kelly.)

However, if the appositive is part of a proper name, or is closely related to the noun or pronoun that it follows, no commas are needed.

Example: My cousin Joan lives in New York.

Example: Eric the Red was a famous Nordic explorer.

EXERCISE 1. Put commas where needed in the following sentences. (Possible Score: 12)

1.   The girl up on the high wire is courageous.

2.   The flag droops limply when there is no wind.

3.   My brother while standing on his head can sing Yankee Doodle Dandy.

4.   The woman driving the red car is my mother.

5.   Peter Sellers who starred in many movies was a fine comedian.

6.   Seeing the storm clouds gathering the boy ran home.

7.   Joe Schmidt who just signed a contract is now the highest paid player in baseball.

8.   The girl who sells the most tickets gets a prize.

9.   The Grand Tetons located in Wyoming are the most beautiful mountain range in my opinion.

10.   Bob Stewart who works for the Telephone Company goes to our church.

Answers are on page 143. Subtract one point for each incorrect answer. *Your Score:* ___

EXERCISE 2. <u>Put commas where needed</u> in the following sentences. (Possible Score: 13)

1.   When she came to visit us we were not home.

2.   If you expect to succeed you must work hard.

3.   Edgar Allen Poe who wrote "The Raven" is a great American poet.

4.   My cousin George lives in Indiana.

5.   "Keep on doing my work" Jesus said "until I return."

6.   Those who work will get paid.

7.   The young man playing the trumpet is my nephew Pat.

8.   We found seaweed in the water on the sand under the rocks and even in our shoes.

9.   The pitcher thinking the batter had struck out headed off the field.

10.   Susanne cramming for the math test wished she had studied harder.

Answers are on page 143. Subtract one point for each incorrect answer. *Your Score:* ___

EXERCISE 3. <u>Put commas where needed</u> in the following sentences. (Possible Score: 12)

1.   The mountain high and majestic shone starkly white against the blue morning sky.

2.   Geronomo a mighty Native American warrior fought many bloody wars.

3.   My sister Eileen has a very beautiful voice.

4.   Martin Luther King's motto "We Shall Overcome" became the rallying cry of the civil rights movement.

5.   Attila the Hun was a barbarian invader.

6.   Mr. Armstrong the county agent spoke to our agriculture class.

7.   I'd like you to meet my nephew Dan.

8.   The Kentucky Colonel owner of a great stud farm won the last Kentucky Derby.

9.   William Shakespeare the author of many famous plays was equally known for his sonnets.

10.   Jimmy the Greek was well known for making odds on just about anything.

Answers are on page 143. Subtract one point for each incorrect answer. *Your Score:* ___

APPLICATION. Write 10 sentences using commas in a variety of ways. Underline the commas in each sentence.

1._____

2._____

3._____

4._____

5._____

6._____

7._____

8._____

9._____

10._____

REVIEW OF FOUNDATION XV

EXERCISE 1. In the sentences below, <u>put commas</u> in the <u>proper places</u>. (Possible Score: 24)

1.   Well I have thought about your offer but must refuse.

2.   Sam would you pick up my dry cleaning on your way home from work/

3. Harry my barber always has a good story to tell.

4. "Where are we going?" Nicole asked.

5. Every Tom Dick and Harry has been calling me this morning.

6. Address the letter: Dear Betty and send it to her in Midland Georgia.

7. On December 14 2003 I will be finishing my exams packing my clothes and heading home for Christmas vacation.

8. My name is listed under Hession Patrick in the telephone directory.

9. Yes I will go with you to the play.

10. My Aunt Mary who lives in Nashville Tennessee is coming to visit us this fall.

11. Mr. Harrison the auctioneer was known affectionately as Louie the Lip.

12. The man who is publishing my book needs the manuscript soon.

13. John Wayne who starred in hundreds of movies was loved by everyone who knew him.

14. Her skirt was made up of red yellow orange green and blue stripes.

15. My cousin found me at work when she came to spend the day with me.

Answers are on page 144. Subtract one point for each incorrect answer. *Your Score:* ___

EXERCISE 2. In the sentences below, <u>put commas in the proper places</u>. (Possible Score: 13)

1. We were married on November 2 1974.

2. We saw tall green majestic mountains.

3. Winds come from the north the east the south and the west.

4. "It is time" she said "for me to go."

5. Billy the Kid was a notorious outlaw.

6.   Wishing to get a better view of the parade we climbed the hill overlooking the route.

7.   Yes you may leave if you have finished your assignment.

8.   Hearing the thunder the boy raced home.

9.   The Himalayas the highest mountains in the world are covered with mighty glaciers.

10.   Athletes who are determined to win must work very hard.

Answers are on page 144. Subtract one point for each incorrect answer. *Your Score:* ___

ANSWERS TO FOUNDATION XV

Exercise 1
exclaimed, "How
Well, if
Now, where
Baxter, Jerry
Seymore, Georgia
10, 2002
grocery, pay
bills, and
"No, I
home, Jack
Oh, go
tomorrow,"
Argentina, Brazil
Brazil, Chile
Chile, Peru
Peru, Bolivia
Bolivia, and

Exercise 2
came, we
saw, we
Ah, well
well, I
Charlie, will
Seymore, Indiana
25, 1939

PHRASES AND CLAUSES/APPOSITIVES

Exercise 1
brother, while
head, can
Sellers, who

Exercise 2
us, we
succeed, you
Poe, who

Exercise 3
mountain, high
majestic, shone
Geronomo, a

movies, was
gathering, the
Schmidt, who
contract, is
Tetons, located
Wyoming, are
range, in
Stewart, who
Company, goes

Raven", is
work," Jesus
said, "until
water, on
sand, under
rocks, and
pitcher, thinking
out, headed
Susanne, cramming
test, wished

warrior, fought
motto, "We
Overcome",
Armstrong, the
agent, spoke
Colonel, owner
farm, won
Shakespeare, the
plays, was

REVIEW

Exercise 1
Well, I
Sam, would
Harry, my
barber, always
Tom, Dick
Dick, Harry
Betty, and
Midland, Georgia
14, 2003
exams, packing
clothes, and
Hession, Patrick
Yes, I
Mary, who
Nashville, Tennessee
Tennessee, is
Harrison, the
auctioneer, was
Wayne, who
movies, was
red, yellow
yellow, orange
orange, green,
green, and

Exercise 2
2, 1974
tall, green
green, majestic
north, the
east, the
south, and
time," she
said, "for
parade, we
Yes, you
thunder, the
Himalayas, the
world, are

ENGLISH FOUNDATIONS

FOUNDATION XVI

OTHER PUNCTUATION

A **COLON** (:) is used after the greeting in a business letter.

Example: To Whom It May Concern:

A colon is used to introduce a list, or an example.

Example: When you go to the store, pick up the following items: potatoes, peanut butter, bread, and milk.

A colon is used to separate the hours from the minutes when you are writing time.

Example: We got home at 9:00 a.m.

EXERCISE. Put a colon I the proper place in the following sentences. (Possible Score: 17)

1. The flight will be leaving at 0700.

2. Here are the courses you will take this year Math, Science, English, History, and Literature.

3. Dear Mr. President

   I am writing to you about the current energy shortage….

4. I will wake you up at 730 tomorrow

5. A good first-aid kit includes the following band-aids, antiseptic cream, sunburn lotion, gauze, iodine, and a small scissors.

6. Marry arrived at 615 this morning.

7. At the farmers market we bought the following fruits apples, peaches, pears, and grapes.

8. We saw the following birds out our window Baltimore orioles, bluebirds, robins, and cardinals.

9. The following schedule will be observed breakfast at 730, seminars at 900 and 1100, lunch at 1230, seminars at 200 and 400, and supper at 600.

10. Please bring the following items with you towels, washcloths, swimsuit, and personal items.

Answers are on page 159. Subtract one point for each incorrect answer. *Your Score:* ___

APPLICATION. Write 5 sentences using colons correctly.

1._____

2._____

3._____

4._____

5._____

A **HYPHEN** (-) is used between parts of a compound word.

    Example: Meet my brother-in-law.

    Example: He was twenty-nine yesterday.

A hyphen is used between syllables of a word that is carried over from the end of a line to the next line.

    Example: In the dictionary, you will find the pro-
    per meaning and spelling of words.

Fractions are hyphenated when they are used as modifiers.

    Example: One-half of the book is finished.

    Example: The bus is two-thirds full.

    Example: The President won by a two-thirds majority.

EXERCISE. Put a hyphen in the proper place or places in the following sentences. (Possible Score: 14)

1.   People living in this neighborhood are generally well to do.

2.   People who complain don't realize it is their responsi
    bility to help stop crime by getting involved in testifying.

3. People who hand you a ten dollar bill for a forty five cent purchase don't realize how trouble
some they are.

4. It is everybody's goal to be self supporting.

5. My boss often acts like a hard hearted employer, but he is really self effacing and merely concerned to get fair treatment from his employees.

6. The Roman Empire was far flung at its highest point.

7. Eighty five percent of people surveyed considered themselves to be above average.

8. In his office, the manager was generally well liked.

9. When it is necessary to divide a word at the end of a line, the divis
ion should be made between syllables, and a hyphen should be placed at the end of the line.

10. Wealthy people are often said to be well heeled.

Answers are on page 159. Subtract one point for each incorrect answer. *Your Score:* ___

APPLICATION. Write 5 sentences using hyphens correctly.

1._____

2._____

3._____

4._____

5._____

An **APOSTROPHE** (') is used to show ownership or possession.

Example: That is Chip's bicycle.

Example: It is Sarah's job to take out the trash after supper.

An apostrophe is used in contractions to take the place of the missing letter or letters.

Example: Don't play in the water. (Don't is a contraction of do not)

Example: It's never too late to change your mind. (It's is a contraction of it is)

If a singular or plural noun does not end in **S**, use an apostrophe and **S** to show ownership or possession.

Example: We are going to Mary's house for supper.

The children's picnic will be held Saturday.

If a singular or plural noun ends in **S**, use an apostrophe only after the **S**.

Example: James' report card was excellent.

Example: I get two weeks' vacation this year.

If two nouns are used to indicate common ownership, put the **'S** or **'** after the second noun.

Example: Bob and Doris' house is up for sale.

Example: Have you seen my sister and brother-in-law's new boat?

If two nouns show separate ownership, put the **'S** or **'** after each noun.

Example: This car is John's and that one is Frances'.

Example: Firemen's and policemen's pensions differ slightly.

EXERCISE. Put the **'** or **'S** in the proper place in the following sentences. (Possible Score: 18)

1. It doesnt matter to me whether we go to Ted and Carols apartment or to the beach.

2. There is a sale on boys suits today.

3. Girls and boys recesses are held at the same time.

4. Nothing is so beautiful as a birds song.

5.   The teachers and the administrators cars are parked in separate places on the parking lot.

6.   Couldnt you help me with the chores?

7.   Sometimes there is little difference between childrens and adults games.

8.   A days wages dont go very far in todays economy.

9.   My mother and fathers income tax was late arriving, and they couldnt understand why.

10.   Those hens eggs are brown, while these ducks eggs are white.

Answers are on page 159. Subtract one point for each incorrect answer. *Your Score:* ___

APPLICATION. Write 5 sentences using apostrophes correctly.

1._____

2._____

3._____

4._____

5._____

A **PERIOD** (.) goes at the end of a sentence that makes a statement.

Example: I will swing by and see you on my way home.

A period goes at the end of a sentence that commands or requests.

Example: Go and get me the wrench out of the tool box.

Example: Please pick up the mail from the mail room.

A period goes after most abbreviations.

Example: Dr. Metcalf is an oral surgeon.

Example: Mr. and Mrs. Jones have invited us to their home.

A period goes after an initial.

Example: P. J. Mortenhouse was a famous inventor.

Three periods are used to show that a quotation is incomplete.

Example: "He did his best . . . yet he never quite succeeded."

A period is used between the integral and decimal parts of a mixed fraction and between figures that indicate dollars and cents.

Example: This road is 75.25 miles from here to the next town.

Example: After the discount, that item cost $13.50.

EXERCISE. In the following sentences, <u>put</u> a <u>period</u> in the <u>proper place</u>. (Possible Score: 17)

1.   Sandra went to Hawaii last summer

2.   The letter was dated Nov 28, 1936

3.   I would like you to pick up your room

4.   Come to the office after school

5.   We shop a lot at J C Penney's

6.   Sam went to Australia last summer

7.   Let me see your new dress

8.   This dinner out cost me $7566

9.   I am told that the lake is 2535 miles long

10.   Please ship that to me COD

Answers are on page 159. Subtract one point for each incorrect answer. *Your Score:* ___

APPLICATION. Write 5 sentences using periods correctly.

1._____

2._____

3._____

4._____

5._____

A **QUESTION MARK** (?) goes at the end of a sentence that asks a question.

     Example: How are you this morning, Mrs. Hamilton?

A question mark goes after the question that is not a complete sentence.

     Example: Why? When?

EXERCISE. Put a question mark in the proper place in the following sentences. (Possible Score: 10)

1.   "Are you going to the convocation" asked John.

2.   You said you wouldn't like this job. Why not

3.   Every good news story answers Who, What, When, Where, Why, and How.

4.   "Are you coming" Susie asked rather impatiently.

5.   Why can't I go to the movie this afternoon

Answers are on page 159. Subtract one point for each incorrect answer. *Your Score:* ___

APPLICATION. Write 5 sentences using question marks correctly.

1._____

2._____

3._____

4._____

5._____

An **EXCLAMATION POINT** (!) goes at the end of any sentence that would be spoken with sudden or sharp emphasis.

> Example: Help! Help!

> Example: Call the police now!

EXERCISE. Put an exclamation point in the proper place in the following sentences. (Possible Score: 6)

1.   "We must run for cover" the captain shouted as the shooting started.

2.   "Ouch   That needle hurts"

3.   Who do you think you are

4.   Jenny, come here this instant

5.   Don't you ever try that again

Answers are on page 160. Subtract one point for each incorrect answer. *Your Score:* ___

APPLICATION. Write 5 sentences using exclamation points correctly.

1._____

2._____

3._____

4._____

5._____

A **DIRECT QUOTATION** says the very same words as the speaker used. The direct quotation is always boxed in by quotation marks (") and always begins with a capital letter.

Example: "Team," said the coach, "You will have to play your very best to win today."

Example: "I don't remember," she said, "Whether I have met you before or not."

The direct quotation is set apart from all other words by a comma, a question mark, or an exclamation point.

Example: "Help!" the swimmer shouted. "I can't swim!"

Example: "What are you doing?" asked Mary.

Example: "Paula," asked Marie, "Have you seen my bracelet anywhere?"

Start a new paragraph each time the speaker changes.

Example: "John, did you plan to get here this early?" asked Susan.

"No, Susan," said John, "But I was able to get an earlier flight."

EXERCISE. <u>Put quotation marks</u> in the <u>proper places</u> in the following sentences. (Possible Score: 28)

1.   Lorna said, Let's ride our bikes to the park.

2.   How hot that soup is! exclaimed Bobby.

3.   Are you a good swimmer? Margaret asked.

4.   What time, asked Stanley, should we leave?

5.   Are we having a meeting today? asked Marsha.

      Yes, at 3:30, Joan answered.

6.   Tom shouted, I made all A's!

7.   Where are you going? asked Anne.

8.   June, I know you will do well with your recital tonight, said Mrs. Weaver.

Thanks for your confidence in me and your encouragement, June responded. I really appreciate it.

9.   I'm hungry! exclaimed David.

10.   We have blood cells in our body, replied Jim, answering the question.

Answers are on page 160. Subtract one point for each incorrect answer. *Your Score:* ___

APPLICATION. Write 5 sentences using quotation marks correctly.

1._____

2._____

3._____

4._____

5._____

SEMICOLONS (;) are used before words like **THEREFORE, HENCE, NEVERTHELESS, HOWEVER, ACCORDINGLY, THUS, THEN, FOR EXAMPLE, FOR INSTANCE, THAT IS, BESIDES, MOREOVER, FURTHERMORE, OTHERWISE, CONSEQUENTLY,** and **HENCE** when they join two independent clauses in a compound sentence.

Example: I flunked my test; therefore, I have to take it again.

Example: My wife decided not to go with me to the ballgame; instead, she stayed home and painted.

If independent clauses in a sentence are <u>not</u> joined by **AND, BUT, OR, NOR, FOR,** or **YET**, use a semicolon between the clauses.

Example: On his last voyage, Henry Hudson was accompanied by his son John; both men were victims of their crew's mutiny.

Use semicolons between clauses that are joined by conjunctions if the clauses are long or if the clauses have commas within themselves.

Example: John arrived last night, I am told; but, because was late, he could not come to the party.

EXERCISE. <u>Put semicolons</u> in the <u>proper places</u> in the following sentences. (Possible Score: 12)

1. The survivors of Hudson's mutinous crew were brought to trial in England the outcome of that trial is unknown.

2. I waited for three hours nevertheless, she never showed up.

3. At our reunion were Mamie, from Boston Sam, who now lives in Houston and my old flame, Hattie, who lives in Hollywood, Florida.

4. A hush fell over the crowd we watched expectantly.

5. Energy sources are running out nevertheless, may will find alternative sources when he is forced to.

6. We invited Jane Jones, the president of the club Sandra Day, the secretary and Jack Jackson, the chairman of the board for supper at our house.

7. Lions were on the loose however, we did not panic but stayed calm.

8. Benjamin Franklin is one of the founders of our country moreover, he was also an author and a scientist.

9. The early Christians refused to worship the Roman emperor as a god therefore, they were persecuted and put to death.

10. Millions of people never attended an opera in their life nevertheless, they are familiar with melodies such as Verdi's "Anvil Chorus."

Answers are on page 160. Subtract one point for each incorrect answer. *Your Score:* ____

APPLICATION. Write 5 sentences using semicolons correctly.

1._____

2._____

3._____

4._____

5._____

REVIEW OF FOUNDATION XVI

EXERCISE 1. Put the <u>proper punctuation marks where they belong</u> in the following sentences. (Possible Score: 48)

Maureen said Come upstairs to my apartment Rudy I want to show you my new puppy

Rudy answered I cant right now I have to babysit for my little brother my mother needs to go shopping Can I come and see your puppy after supper

Yes do and you can bring your brother too if you wish replied Maureen

I dont think I should He has a cold and I dont think my mother would like him to go out of the apartment said Rudy

Well you come alone then What time will you be able to come asked Maureen

Will 700 be all right asked Rudy

Great Ill see you then said Maureen

Answers are on page 160. Subtract one point for each incorrect answer. *Your Score:* ___

EXERCISE 2. Put the <u>proper punctuation marks where they belong</u> in the following sentences. (Possible Score: 16)

13681 Hwy 16N

Millers Creek NC 28651

June 21 2004

Black Mall Book Store

1818 W Fourth St

New York NY 10012

Dear Sirs

I would like to order a copy of each of the following *Huckleberry Finn* by Mark Twain *Little Women* by Louisa May Alcott and *Travels with Charlie* by John Steinbeck I am enclosing a money order for $4500

Sincerely yours

Penny Hession

Answers are on page 160. Subtract one point for each incorrect answer. *Your Score:* ___

EXERCISE 3. <u>Put</u> the <u>proper punctuation marks where they belong</u> in the following sentences. (Possible Score: 71)

1.   Ill meet you promptly at 720 at Fifty eighth Street and Regal Court said Roger Be sure youre there on time

2.   The Lafayette *Chronicle* the Smiths hometown newspaper has an article about them its very informative

3.   The following students scored over ninety five on last weeks test Linda Tom Ken and Priscilla

4.   I dont think said Mark that you've read the short story I gave you

5.   When I asked the time did you say 540 or 545

6.   Joe said that his father owned two thirds of the company while Mr Perry had a one fifth share

7.   Tony said he would attend the meeting however Fred shouted I wont go

8.   My favorite painting is Van Goghs *Sunflower in a Vase*

9.   Hogans face shone as he exclaimed Ive found the deers tracks moreover Ive

caught sight of the deer

10. He listed the planets nearest the sun as follows Mercury Venus Earth and Mars

Answers are on page 160. Subtract one point for each incorrect answer. *Your Score:* ___

ANSWERS TO FOUNDATION XVI

COLONS	HYPHENS	APOSTROPHES
Exercise	**Exercise**	**Exercise**
07:00	well-to-do	doesn't
year:	responsi-bility	Carol's
President:	ten-dollar	boys'
7:30	forty-five	Girls'
following:	trouble-some	boys'
6:15	self-supporting	bird's
following:	hard-hearted	teachers'
window:	self-effacing	administrators'
observed:	far-flung	Couldn't
7:30	Eighty-five	children's
9:00	well-liked	adults'
11:00	divis-ion	day's
12:30	well-heeled	don't
2:00		today's
4:00		father's
6:00		couldn't
you:		hens'
		ducks'

PERIODS	QUESTION MARKS
Exercise	**Exercise**
summer.	convocation?"
Nov.	not?

1936.
room.
school.
J. C.
Penney's.
summer.
dress.
$75.66.
25.35
long.
C.O.D.

Who?
What?
When?
Where?
Why?
How?
coming?"
afternoon?

EXCLAMATION POINT

Exercise
Cover!"
Ouch!
Hurts!
are!
instant!
again!

Exercise
England;
hours;
Boston;
Houston;
crowd;
out;
club;
secretary;
loose;
country;
god;
life;

DIRECT QUOTATION

Exercise
"Let's
park."
"How
is!"
"Are
swimmer?"
"What
time,"
"should
leave?"
"Are
today?"
"Yes,
3:30,"
"I
A's!"
"Where
going?"
"June
tonight,"
"Thanks
encouragement,
"I
"I
it."
"I'm

hungry!"
"We
body."

REVIEW

Exercise 1

said,
"Come
apartment,
Rudy.
puppy."
answered,
"I
can't
now.
baby-sit
brother;
shopping.
supper?"
"Yes,
do,
brother,
too,
wish,"
Maureen.
"I
don't
should.
cold,
don't
apartment,"
Rudy.
"Well,
then.
come?"
Maureen.
"Will
7:00
right?"
Rudy.
"Great!

Exercise 2

Hwy.
Creek,
21,
W.
St.
York,
Sirs:
following:
Finn,
Twain,
Women,
Alcott;
Charlie,
Steinbeck.
$45.00.
yours,

Exercise 3

"I'll
7:20
Fifty-eighth
Court,"
Roger.
"Be
you're
time."
Chronicle,
Smith's
home-town
newspaper.
them;
it's
informative.
ninety-five
week's
test:
Linda,
Tom,
Ken,
Priscilla.
"I
don't
think,"
Mark,
"that
you've
you."
"When
time,
5:40
5:45?"

two-thirds

"I'll
then,"
Maureen.

company,
Mr.
one-fifth
share.
meeting;
"however,"
shouted,
"I
won't
go!"
Gogh's
Vase.
Hogan's
exclaimed,
"I've
deer's
tracks;
moreover,
I've
deer!"
follows:
Mercury,
Venus,
Earth,
Mars.